TEQUILA & TACOS

TEQUILA

& TACOS

A GUIDE TO SPIRITED PAIRINGS

KATHERINE COBBS

TILLER PRESS

New York London Toronto Sydney New Delhi

TILLER PRESS

An Imprint of Simon & Schuster, Inc.
1230 Avenue of the Americas
New York, NY 10020

First Tiller Press hardcover edition April 2020

TILLER PRESS and colophon are trademarks of Simon & Schuster, Inc.

For information about special discounts for bulk purchases, please contact Simon & Schuster Special Sales at 1-866-506-1949 or business@simonandschuster.com.

The Simon & Schuster Speakers Bureau can bring authors to your live event. For more information or to book an event contact the Simon & Schuster Speakers Bureau at 1-866-248-3049 or visit our website at www.simonspeakers.com.

Conceived and produced by Blueline Creative Group LLC.
Visit: www.bluelinecreativegroup.com
Concept and copy by Katherine Cobbs
Interior Design by Matt Ryan
Photography by Becky Luigart-Stayner
Food Styling by Torie Cox
Prop Styling by Mindi Shapiro
Recipe Development and Testing by Katherine Cobbs, Lyda Burnette, and Ferrell Carter
Book Trailer by Ellie Stayner

Manufactured in the United States of America

10 9 8 7 6 5

Library of Congress Cataloging-in-Publication Data

Names: Cobbs, Katherine, author.
Title: Tequila & tacos : a guide to spirited pairings / Katherine Cobbs.
Description: New York : Tiller Press, 2020. | Series: Spirited pairings; book 2 | Includes index.
Identifiers: LCCN 2019046229 (print) | LCCN 2019046230 (ebook) | ISBN 9781982137595 (hardcover) | ISBN 9781982137601 (ebook)
Subjects: LCSH: Cocktails. | Cooking, Mexican. | Restaurants—United States—Directories. | LCGFT: Cookbooks.
Classification: LCC TX951 .C614 2020 (print) | LCC TX951 (ebook) | DDC 641.87/4—dc23
LC record available at https://lccn.loc.gov/2019046229
LC ebook record available at https://lccn.loc.gov/2019046230

ISBN 978-1-9821-3759-5
ISBN 978-1-9821-3760-1 (ebook)

I am grateful to Mexico for its innumerable culinary gifts—chiles, tortillas, agave spirits, chocolate, vanilla, and so much more deliciousness—but mostly for its beautiful people. May these gifts keep coming.

To my husband, John, a curator of Mexican hot sauces. After twenty-five years, I am learning not to take personally the spicy blanket you cover every dish with before you've even taken a bite. You keep life spicy and always fun. Xo

CONTENTS

INTRODUCTION

My maiden tequila experience is too typical: Late '80s, high school spring break. Cancun. Tourist hole-in-the-wall. No ID required. Catering to the clientele, bartenders served tequila in Day-Glo toilet bowl–size margaritas, or as shots to be slammed in one cringe-worthy gulp after a lick of salt or a sweaty neck, with the requisite lime-wedge pacifier to quell any potential heave. Thank God there were no cell phones back then. The experience had zero to do with taste, any way you define it. It was a means to an end. In those days, tequila (if what was poured even was tequila) was maligned or misused by bar goer and bartender alike, and north of the border it was mostly misunderstood.

My introduction to tacos was considerably tamer. I can't say when I first sampled one, but as the child of proud Texans who summered at a family cabin in the mountains of northeastern New Mexico, I'd like to say it was something authentic and special. Instead, what I remember is that whether I was at home, the school cafeteria, a fast-food drive-thru or a mom-and-pop Mexican restaurant, tacos all came the same way—a canoe of crisp corn cradling taco-seasoned meat, shredded cheese, a nest of lettuce, cubes of tomato, sour cream, and the redundant "spicy picante sauce" that was rarely that. I considered it fancy if a few sliced black olives appeared. Now, I won't lie. I really liked those tacos as I did sloppy Joes and Frito pie. They were greasy, savory, simple, and satisfying in a way I can still appreciate. My parents raised their eyebrows when I ordered tacos at restaurants like Santa Fe's Pink Adobe or Lambert's of Taos, so I would demur and order the green chile stew or blue corn enchiladas instead. If we were at Mexican Inn Cafe or Joe T. Garcia's in Dad's hometown of Fort Worth, I was urged to "be more adventurous" than a taco. Catering to American tastes then, these gringo tacos (anglicized versions of Mexico's rolled and fried *tacos dorados*) were like chicken fingers . . . mostly all the same.

After college in Texas and a handful of years in DC, I spent the rest of the '90s living in San Francisco attending culinary school, working for a cookbook publisher, and helping launch one of the first major cooking websites. My decade there revolved around food and too much fun. Burritos were the thing . . . big fat daddies from favorite spots like Gordo's on Clement, Zona Rosa on Haight, or Taqueria Cancun in the Mission. They were easily two full-size meals rolled in a manhole-size flour tortilla, but so delicious and dangerously easy to devour before their immense size registered in your stomach. It was just too much, so I started

ordering tacos. These weren't the tacos of my childhood, they were classic Mexican street tacos: small corn tortillas griddled on a smoking *comal*, topped with meat, queso fresco, nuggets of raw white onion, and a scattering of cilantro leaves. Have one or three. Order as you go. After my years mastering the art of French cooking at Tante Marie's Cooking School and working on a stream of fancy cookbooks, these tacos were a necessary reminder of how the thoughtful combination of just a few ingredients can be quite deliciously enough. To me the taco is meal perfection.

Skip ahead to the new century, my friend and former colleague was regularly teaching cooking classes at Rancho La Puerta, a chic spa on the Baja Peninsula. She tagged me as her free plus-one a couple of times, which was like winning the luxe lotto. One trip, a few of us ventured off the ranch and into the town of Tecate for an authentic Mexican meal at the restaurant Asao. It was there I experienced my first tequila flight—a sampling of one maker's blanco, reposado, and añejo tequilas. Wait, THIS was tequila?! Sensing my enthusiasm, I suppose, the waiter delivered a shallow clay *copita* brimming with mezcal—mostly ordered by locals then. With one resinous, woodsy sip, a portal to a spirited new frontier had been opened for me to explore.

Chalk it up to star chefs, food television, farm-to-table, or eat-out culture, but today tequila and tacos are riding a tsunami. Agave spirits are sipped, savored, sought, and collected. Flights are poured and flavor notes pondered. Distillers tinker with technique and taste and keep methods top secret. Tequilerias and mezcalerias are becoming as common as whiskey and wine bars. And like never before, bartenders are building inventive cocktails using both familiar and lesser known agave spirits—tequila, mezcal, raicilla, bacanora, sotol, and pulque—that highlight rather than mask agave's distinctive flavors.

I'd venture to guess that as salsa displaced ketchup as the reigning condiment in America in the 1990s, tacos eclipsed hot dogs as America's favorite street food long ago too—if not in actual volume, certainly in popular fashion. Whether eaten out of hand from a corner cart or enjoyed after a long-awaited reservation, today we have the luxury of finding tacos served any way we like: wrapped in a corn tortilla, flour tortilla, or a gluten-free, grain-free, paleo, keto lettuce leaf. We can take the traditional trail with al pastor, guisado, barbacoa, or carnitas fillings, follow a fine-dining path with short rib, Brussels sprout, or lobster tacos, or go for a global spin and relish salmon poke in a crisp nori shell or curried cauliflower folded in Indian paratha bread. Throughout this book you will sometimes find a specific brand of product noted or distiller called out. Know that this is the preference of the chef or bartender who contributed the recipe. Always feel free to use whatever brands of these ingredients and products you prefer.

Though I am an expert of nothing, I am a lifelong gustatory adventurer willing to try pretty much anything. And if I love something, I soak up all I can about it, sample it wherever I find it, learn how to make it, and love sharing it. That's what these Guides to Spirited Pairings are all about—honing in on what's hot in the world of food and drink, discovering the people and places doing delicious things in a category, and then collecting their stories and recipes so that anyone can re-create and experience the drink and dish. Today, the world truly is your taco. I say enjoy it with a cocktail.

Salud!

TEQUILA TALK

To understand tequila, it helps to get a handle on agave spirits as a whole. For the purposes of this book, tequila and the array of other spirits made through the fermentation and/or distillation of agave varieties or relatives are included on the pages that follow. The history of these spirits is long, rich, and varied. For a deep dive, check out the resources in my Resources section (page 156).

WHAT IS TEQUILA?

Tequila is mezcal made from the distillation of a single variety of steam-cooked agave (or century plant), the blue Weber agave. Most tequila is produced in the lowland and highland areas of the Mexican state of Jalisco, but four other states—Guanajuato, Michoacán, Nayarit, and Tamaulipas—are also recognized by the international Appellation of Origin (AO) and Mexico's Denomination of Origin. Blue agave for tequila is pressure-cooked, typically in clay or copper ovens, which does not infuse the tequila with additional flavor during processing. Bottled tequila can be made from as little as 51% agave sugar mixed with a blend of other sugars (called Mixto) or from 100% agave, which is what you should buy at the liquor store and request at the bar.

Tequila is either bottled right after distillation or aged. Aged tequilas are rested in French or American oak barrels, including spent bourbon, whiskey, wine, or cognac barrels. The type of barrel a distiller uses influences the finished flavor profile of the tequila. There are five expressions of tequila to remember—from youngest to oldest and lightest to darkest.

BLANCO OR PLATA: unaged tequila that remains clear and is bottled soon after distillation. The best of these have peppery brightness and retain the distinctive notes of agave.

JOVEN: this blanco tequila is either aged a few weeks or blended with aged tequila to develop a more nuanced flavor.

REPOSADO: aged at least two months or up to one year, this tequila is golden (not to be confused with "Gold Tequila," which has added color) and has hints of sweetness and spice.

AÑEJO: aged a minimum of one year, but less than three years, to give the tequila a layered complexity of taste from agave, oak, and the residual flavor notes of whatever liquid was aged in the barrel previously.

EXTRA AÑEJO: aged at least three years, these long-rested tequilas reflect the flavors of the host barrel most distinctively.

WHAT IS MEZCAL?

Think of mezcal as the precursor to tequila, and both root and branch of the distilled agave spirits category. Any spirit, including tequila, that is the distilled fermentation of any of the three dozen or so unique varieties of the genus *Agave* is "at its root" mezcal. Agave that are traditionally baked in earthen pits over wood take on the distinctive smoky notes we've come to associate with the "branch of spirits" we think of mezcal. Like champagne, mezcal was granted an AO, which means that distillations of agave can only be labeled "mezcal" when produced in one of eight Mexican states—Durango, Guanajuato, Guerrero, Michoacán, Puebla, San Luis Potosí, and Zacatecas, with the majority produced in Oaxaca.

The largest percentage of mezcal is produced from the cultivation of the espadin varietal. A handful of other cultivars are also used, as well as wild plants foraged within the official states. As for wine, the agave varietal used is the biggest flavor differentiator, but age matters too. There are three main styles on the market. The most common by far is joven (unaged), but "rested" or reposado (rested in oak less than a year), and añejo (aged up to three years) can also be found.

THEN WHAT THE HECK ARE AGAVE SPIRITS?

In addition to tequila and mezcal, there are other spirits distilled from plants in the broad family *Agavoideae* that have different names for different reasons:

- Agave-based spirits like bacanora that are produced outside designated AO territories cannot be labeled "mezcal."

- Spirits produced from non-agave species cannot be called mezcal, such as sustainable sotol made from the desert spoon plant, which is "officially" produced in the states of Chihuahua, Coahuila, and Durango.

- Production methods can put a product in its own class. Pulque, a viscous, milky, low-alcohol beverage is made through the fermentation of agave, but it is not distilled. It has a funky, yeasty flavor reminiscent of beer. Consider this ancient elixir the precursor to mezcal, as it is likely the oldest alcoholic agave beverage around.

- In the case of raicilla, all these things—origin, plant type, and production method—keep it from getting either a mezcal or tequila designation. Unlike mezcal, raicilla is made by roasting agave in clay ovens rather than over wood in earthen pits, resulting in a liquor embedded with earthiness without smoke, and it is finished via single-distillation versus mezcal's double-distillation. Finally, because it is made outside the designated states where mezcal must originate, it cannot be labeled mezcal. Though raicilla is produced like tequila and in the state of Jalisco, because it is made from *Agave Raicilla* or *Agave Maximiliana* instead of blue Weber agave, it cannot be labeled "tequila" either.

FROM FIELD TO BOTTLE

Agave plants are monocarpic, reproducing once before dying. *Jimadors* (farmers) regularly cut off the asparagus-like flower stalk, or *quiote*, that the plant sends up as a calling card for long-nosed bats to feed on its nectar and fertilize it after dark. Cutting off the quiote before it grows keeps nutrients in the plant and encourages the base to fatten with sugar. This cultivation practice has created problems for bats and agave diversity (see Resources, page 156).

When it is time to harvest agave for distillation, the jimador cuts away the leaves. A leafless heart, or *piña*, laden with sweet sap can weigh in at one hundred pounds or more. The piñas are either steamed in brick ovens called "hornos" or steel autoclaves for tequila with unadulterated agave flavor, or they are roasted over wood in earthen pits called *palenques* for mezcal. The roasting process imbues the piñas with flavorful wisps of wood smoke and the caramelized notes of tobacco, coffee bean, and toasted dry chile. Both cooking techniques convert complex sugars into fermentable ones.

The cooked piñas must be crushed to extract the *aguamiel*, or "honey water," for fermentation. Mechanical crushers commonly do the job at modern tequila distilleries, while a millstone and grinding wheel pulled by a mule, ox, or horse do the work for mezcal.

The tequila fermentation process is kicked off with the addition of yeast to the fermentation tank. A few days later the liquid is transferred to a pot still or stainless steel column still to be distilled. Mezcal fermentation enlists mother nature to inoculate vats or wooden barrels with airborne yeast—a process that may take a week or so. The resulting mash is then double-distilled in pot stills or copper stills.

When distillation is complete, tequila and mezcal are bottled right away for an unaged product or transferred to barrels to rest for reposado or hibernate for añejo bottlings.

In Mexico, both tequila and mezcal are traditionally served neat to prime the appetite before a meal, or to be sipped and savored with it. However, these spirits do play well with others, so try unaged varieties in cocktails you would normally mix up with vodka or gin and look to aged varieties where brown liquors commonly make an appearance. Get creative, forget the rules, and shake or stir things up any way you like.

TACOS WITHOUT BORDERS

Authenticity has its place . . . like when you want to know that the five-figure engagement ring you bought your girl is an actual diamond and not a knockoff, or that the Babe Ruth baseball card you found in the attic is the real deal that will fund your retirement. Applied to a particular dish or recipe, authenticity is meaningless. It has no place. Every cuisine and every dish is an evolution.

Lebanese immigrants to Veracruz, trying to replicate the flatbread-wrapped lamb shawarma of their homeland, turned to the meat that was available to them right where they were. It just happened to be pork that had been introduced to Mexico by Spanish explorers centuries before. Thinly sliced, marinated, and threaded in compressed layers on a vertical, rotating spit, the tower of meat resembled a top or, as Mexicans called it, a *trompo*. When it was time to eat, the meat was shaved off the tower into succulent shreds and folded in the local flatbread: the Mexican tortilla. So this one shepherd-style, or *al pastor*, taco was born of contributions from the Middle East, Europe and Central America, and created through ingenuity, improvisation, trial-and-error, and a deep desire to satisfy a craving. It has evolved ever since.

That taco origin story exemplifies how we can experience a bit of the world in a single bite, whether it is cloaked in a corn tortilla, sandwiched in a seeded bun, tops a chewy crust, or is called a taco, burger, or pizza. Every iconic dish is a fusion of ingredients, cultures, and creativity, and every time it is made by different hands, it is also a reflection of the cook. The recipes in this book deliciously demonstrate that.

TACO TRADITIONS

Authenticity may be overrated, but history and tradition help us understand the evolution of a cuisine or dish. Though Mexicans had been cradling food in tortillas for ages, it wasn't called a taco until recent times. The word taco, or wedge, was a term Mexican miners used to describe the sticks of dynamite that they wrapped in paper and tucked in crevices to blast rock for ore. One of the earliest mentions of the taco as food was a reference to *tacos mineros*, or miner's tacos, in the late 1800s to note the portable street food of the working classes. Throughout Central and South America, the word "taco" refers to many different things like pool cue, heel of a shoe, a cigarette, an intelligent person, getting inebriated, or bragging. It seems the meanings are as varied as taco combinations. Some may wonder why all the fuss over something as simple as a tortilla wrapped around a filling, but it's the versatility of the taco as a cheap, portable vessel for infinite fillings that made it iconic.

MEXICAN TACOS TRANSLATED

By and large, the recipes in this book are anything but traditional, though many use the classic cooking styles or traditional ingredients found in the tacos listed below. This list just skims the surface.

ALAMBRE: means "wire" and refers to chunks of meat like beef that are commonly skewered with onion, peppers, cheese, and bacon, and grilled for kebabs. The same ingredients are typically sautéed in a skillet together for tacos.

AL CARBON, ASADA, ASADERO: grilled beef steak usually cooked over charcoal or roasted to develop a flavorful char and then thinly sliced.

AL PASTOR, ADOBADA, OR ÁRABES: "shepherd-style" (al pastor) pork slices that have been marinated in red chile adobo sauce (adobada), skewered and roasted on a vertical spit or trompo, and served with pineapple, white onion, and cilantro. It originated as a replication of Lebanese (Árabes) shawarma by immigrants to Veracruz.

BARBACOA: refers to meats that are slow-cooked over an open flame.

BIRRIA: a special-occasion dish of spicy guajillo chile–bathed goat that is stewed until velvety tender.

BISTEC: thinly sliced beef shoulder steak.

CABEZA—MADE FROM PARTS OF AN ANIMAL'S HEAD: buche (bird's crop/esophagus, but also a pig's stomach), cachete (cheeks), lengua (tongue), ojo (eyes), sesos (brain), and trompa (lips), typically served with salsa, onion, and cilantro.

CANASTA, AL VAPOR, OR SUDADOS: quick-fried tortillas topped with a few fillings like cheese, refried beans, chicharrón, or potato that are folded over and layered in a basket (canasta) where they steam (al vapor) so that they are soft and sweaty (sudados). These tacos are traditionally sold by bicycle vendors.

CAZO: translated as "bucket" tacos, these are made by frying meat to order in hot lard in a metal bowl for filling tacos to order.

CAMPECHANOS: tacos layered with several different types of meat, such as marinated grilled beef that has been air-dried (cecina), chicharrón (fried pork belly), and blood sausage, and topped with salsa, white onion, and lime juice.

CARNITAS: translates to "little meats" and typically refers to seasoned pork shoulder that is braised in its own fat until it falls apart and is easily shredded.

CHAPULINES: dried, toasted, and sometimes seasoned grasshoppers that are eaten as a snack or used as a taco garnish.

CHICHARRÓN: deep-fried pig skin with meat attached.

CHIVO: goat meat tacos.

CHORIZO: raw minced pork that is seasoned with chiles and spices and wrapped in intestine casing. The casing is removed to cook the sausage to serve.

COCHINITA PIBIL: suckling pig marinated in citrus, spices, and annatto seed and slow-roasted.

CUERITOS: thin strips of pork skin pickled with vinegar, fruit, spices, and chiles.

DORADOS: traditionally hard shell or rolled tacos (*taquitos* or *flautas*) filled with an array of fillings.

GUISADOS: tacos filled with boggy one-pot stews of slow-cooked braised meats, greens, beans, or vegetables.

HUITLACOCHE: the prized corn fungus that grows on organic ears of corn that is considered the Mexican truffle.

PESCADO AND CAMARONES: a Baja original, fish or shrimp served grilled or fried with shredded lettuce or cabbage, pico de gallo, avocado or guacamole, and crema fresca or citrus-lightened and seasoned mayonnaise.

POLLO: marinated and grilled chicken served diced or shredded with your choice of toppings.

RAJAS: smoky cheese.

RES: denotes beef, so if you see *suadero de res* or *barbacoa de res* on a menu you know what meat you're getting.

SUADERO: slowly braised meat, usually beef cut from the belly, that is pan-fried to crisp up before filling tacos.

TINGA: dark-meat chicken simmered in a chile-tomato sauce and finely shredded or chopped.

TRIPAS: braised beef stomach or simmmered intestine.

TACO TASTES

You can find proof of the taco's versatility as a vehicle for flavorful fillings everywhere these days and in this book. There is no singular formula for taco greatness, but there does seem to be some recurring tastes and textures that lend complexity to this humble handheld.

TORTILLAS: Fresh handmade corn or flour tortillas are critical to a great taco. Shelf-stable tortillas packed with preservatives just don't cut it. Seek out homemade flour tortillas and corn tortillas made from nixtamalized corn masa from a local *tortilleria*, Mexican restaurant, or Latin grocery. Buy them fresh and use them quickly or freeze them to use as needed. Nixtamalization is a process by which dried corn is soaked in an alkaline solution of limewater or wood ash lye, washed, and then hulled. The chemical reaction of the process removes toxins from the grain and improves nutrient density. It also allows the grain, once ground into masa, to come together and form a dough. On the pages that follow, at times a particular size tortilla is called for, and sometimes it is just corn or flour tortillas in general. When the chef who contributed a recipe has a preference, it is noted. Feel free to use whatever type or size of tortilla you prefer.

BASE FILLING: The starring ingredient is a warm, well-seasoned protein, vegetable, or starch that has been stewed, steamed, sautéed, smoked, grilled, pit-roasted, or dried.

SALSA: Spanish for "sauce," the options are as varied as taco types—dried chile salsas, fresh fruit or vegetable salsas, chunky salsas, smooth salsas, mild salsas, and spicy salsas. These are an opportunity to add bright acidity and herbaceousness as a pleasing foil for the base filling.

CREMA: This Mexican sour cream is a cooling counterpoint to warm ingredients, but also the heat of spicy chiles. Crema may also be embellished with ingredients like citrus juices, spices, chiles, and herbs. Sometimes gussied-up mayonnaise figures in.

CHEESE: Whether salty and crumbly, rich and creamy, or melty and stringy, many varieties of cheese are enlisted into action depending on the desired texture and flavor sought (see Know Your Queso, page 17).

GARNISHES: This is a place to get fun with tasty textural counterpoints to the other ingredients. Things like a tangle of lettuce or cabbage, diced tomato, avocado or other fruits, grated white onion, chopped scallion, chopped chiles, radishes and other diced fresh vegetables, as well as nuts or seeds are typical toppers. Pickled ingredients like peppers, sliced onions, radishes, cabbage slaw, and vegetable medleys add bold acidity to prime the palate bite after bite.

KNOW YOUR QUESO

Cheese was introduced to Mexico by the Spanish, who brought dairy animals, too. Most Mexican cheeses are made from fresh cow's milk, though you will stumble upon goat's or sheep's milk cheeses too. There are many specialty cheeses unique to particular Mexican states, but these are the most common found stateside.

AÑEJO: This "aged" queso fresco is firm and salty and has a more pungent and pronounced flavor. It is sometimes found coated in chile paste.

ASADERO: This is a fresh semisoft cheese that melts well and is used in *queso fundido* and quesadillas or where a mild, melting cheese is desired.

BLANCO: A fresh "white" cheese that is milky and mild and like a famer's cheese cross between cottage cheese and mozzarella. It is sometimes called *queso enchilada* or *queso sierra*. It softens rather than melts when heated, so is ideal for holding up in baked dishes like enchiladas.

CHIHUAHUA: A holey, semi-hard cheese made by Mennonites in the Mexican state of the same name. Like cheddar, it can be mild to sharp in flavor.

COTIJA: In Mexico, this dry, aged goat's milk cheese, similar in flavor and texture to parmesan or pecorino, is most often used as a garnish. It is the go-to finishing cheese on *elote*, the grilled Mexican street corn.

FRESCO: This "fresh" spongy cheese is mild and similar to feta or ricotta salata in flavor and texture. It is mostly crumbled and used as a garnish for tacos, baked dishes, corn, and salads.

MANCHEGO: In Spain, this cheese is made with sheep's milk, but fresh Mexican Manchego is made with cow's milk or a blend of cow and goat milks.

OAXACA: A stretched cheese that is formed into braided balls and similar to *queso asadero*. Your go-to for melty, stringy, rich *queso fundido*, this melting cheese is also the standard for quesadillas, chile rellenos, and other gooey favorites.

PANELA: This fresh skim-milk cheese has little fat and holds up to grilling like halloumi cheese from Cyprus. Panela is sometimes molded in baskets and called *queso de canasta*.

PANTRY PEPPERS – DRIED CHILE PRIMER

Chile peppers are powerhouses of Mexican cookery. Just like a grape tastes decidedly different from a raisin, dried chiles are something altogether different from their fresh state. These red or dark staples of the pantry impart unique flavor and varying levels of heat to dishes. Get to know them. They add a whole new world of delicious complexity to whatever you are cooking.

First-step Prep: Before soaking to reconstitute dried chiles, remove the dried stems, shake out the bitter seeds, or scrape them out after soaking. Sometimes dried chiles are toasted in a dry or lightly oiled skillet before soaking to coax out more flavor.

ANCHO: Redolent of raisins and fruit with a slightly smoky quality, these are poblano chiles picked just when they turn red, and then dried. They are the most popular dried chile in Mexico, are mild to moderate in spiciness, and used in marinades, *adobos* (chile pastes), or where rich flavor and color are desired.

ARBOL: Translates to "tree-like pepper," this chile is red with a woody stem and nutty, pungent flavor. Arbol chiles pack a wallop of spicy heat that becomes more pronounced when toasted.

CASCABEL: The name of this deep red, bell-shaped dried pepper translates to "little bell," but it is also called a "rattle chile" for the seeds that rattle inside the dried skin. It is the dried form of a chile bola. Cascabels have a sweet, fruity flavor and minimal heat and are used in soups, stews, and salsas, and serve as a nice complement to corn masa in tamales.

CHIPOTLE: This is a smoked red jalapeño that you can also find canned with adobo sauce, but when it is dried after smoking, it turns a dusty, leathery tan. It has moderate heat and a vibrant, smoky flavor with hints of coffee.

GUAJILLO: Translates to "big pod," these long, thin, rust-red chiles have mild to medium heat and an earthy pungency that is welcome in adobos, stews, and tomato-based sauces. They are rarely used in their fresh form. Due to their tough skins, they require a longer soak than other dried chiles.

MORITA: These lightly smoked red jalapeño peppers have a shiny skin that is mottled with wrinkles. What differentiates this chile from dried chipotles is that they are smoked for less time, which maintains their fruitiness while developing notes of chocolate and tobacco. They are used in moles and salsas.

MULATO: Like anchos, these are dried poblano chiles that are allowed to ripen to their fullest before being harvested and dried, giving more complexity of sweet spice and fruit. They are a classic in mole sauce.

PASILLA OR NEGRO: One name for this chile is derived from the word *pasas* or "raisins." It is a dried chilaca pepper that is moderately hot. Dark, shriveled, and gnarled with a complex caramel-like richness and notes of dried fruit, pasillas are often mixed with other dried chiles and blended into mole sauces.

PEQUIN: Also called Tepin or Bird Chiles, these are ten times spicier than a jalapeño and have the same name fresh or dried. Small green ones are preferred when using fresh, or they are allowed to ripen to red before they are dried. Dried pequin chiles are ground into flakes to use as a seasoning to sprinkle on food or add to chorizo.

WEST

THE RESTAURANTS

BARRIO MEXICAN KITCHEN & BAR

1420 12TH AVENUE
SEATTLE, WA 98122
206.588.8105
BARRIORESTAURANT.COM

Nestled in Seattle's Capitol Hill neighborhood, Barrio is a striking hacienda-style restaurant that feels worlds away from the city's mist and drizzle. Expansive beams and terra-cotta walls infuse the space with a welcoming warmth, while a massive pueblo-inspired kiva fireplace covered in an earthy tile mosaic grounds the soaring space. A curvaceous bar flanked by a wall of flickering pillar candles is a nice vantage point to sip a cocktail and take in the action. There, Bar Manager Maggie DiGiovanni and her bartending companions exude hospitality, guiding imbibers on the finer points of agave spirits. For those who haven't "dipped a toe" in the world of agave spirits, she might recommend a cocktail, but often suggests starting with "a lower proof, lightly smoky Espadin, a second Espadin with a slightly different profile, and then a wild agave selection to give a sense of the depths to explore in the category."

Pop in on Monday nights to keep the exploration going with a flight selected from the one-hundred-plus bottles of tequila and mezcal for half the usual price. Nibble on roasted corn bathed in epazote oil, blanketed with cotija and a dusting of chile pequin, or share a salad of tomato, watermelon, avocado, and crunchy fried quinoa while you peruse the dinner menu.

Born in Zacatecas, Mexico, Chef Frankie Gonzalez began cooking in restaurants as a teenager, honing his craft under the tutelage of Chef Harry Mills of Seattle's Purple Café. At the helm of Barrio, Gonzalez returns to his roots while celebrating his current home by weaving the unique ingredients of the Pacific Northwest into traditional Latin dishes.

When the weather permits, hit Barrio at lunchtime. Step beyond the massive Spanish mission–style doors to the outdoor patio to enjoy the taco special. Pick any two tacos, such as traditional al pastor or chicken tinga or Chef Gonzalez's inventive vegan chorizo made from cashew cheese, which also shows up in Barrio's vegan nachos. For dinner, the kitchen's halibut taco is not to be missed. Tender chunks of the freshest local halibut are topped with a lacy tangle of shaved fennel and red onion and garnished with a bright and tangy citrus aioli made from grilled lemons. Cucumber stands in for the usual tomato in a pico de gallo that lends crunch and another layer of freshness to what is pretty much fish taco perfection.

JARDÍN DE BRUJAS SERVES 1

Bar Manager Maggie DiGiovanni recommends using an Espadin mezcal with a bright profile in this cocktail, such as Wahaka or Agave de Cortes.

1½ ounces Espadin mezcal

⅓ ounce Giffard Pamplemousse

¼ ounce Strega liqueur

½ ounce lemon juice

3 drops of saline solution

1 dash Angostura bitters

1 grapefruit peel strip

2 to 3 mint sprigs

Combine all the ingredients, except the mint, in a Collins glass. Fill with crushed ice and stir with a swizzle stick. Garnish with a large strip of grapefruit peel and bundled mint sprigs.

WHAT'S IN A NAME?

This "Garden of Witches" cocktail is a nod to the Strega in the recipe— a word for "witch" in Italian. "More abstractly, the way the mezcal plays with the herbal and floral notes of the other ingredients evokes memories of overgrown herb gardens in books that I read as a kid. It's bold, beautiful, mysterious, and maybe a little dangerous," says Maggie.

PAN-SEARED HALIBUT TACO SERVES 2 TO 3

This is a super fresh spin on the classic fish taco that Chef Gonzalez brought with him from the Purple Café. No batter. No cabbage. Instead, crunchy shaved fennel and spicy red onion serve as slaw stand-ins. The requisite creamy drizzle gets a burst of bright flavor from juicy grilled lemon, while the crunch of cucumber surprises in Barrio's pico de gallo. Save the fennel fronds for garnish, if desired.

12 ounces halibut

1 tablespoon canola oil

Kosher salt

1 cup thinly shaved fennel

¼ cup thinly shaved red onion

6 (5½-inch) corn tortillas

½ teaspoon each fennel and coriander seeds, toasted and ground

¼ cup Grilled Lemon Aioli (recipe follows)

1 cup Cucumber Pico de Gallo (recipe follows)

Cilantro leaves

1   Preheat the oven to 500°F. Slice the halibut into 6 (2-ounce) portions.

2   Heat a large cast-iron skillet over medium-high heat. Add the canola oil. Season the fish on both sides with salt and place in the hot pan to sear until golden brown, 1 to 2 minutes. Transfer the pan to the oven for 3 minutes or until just cooked through.

3   Divide the fennel and red onion between 6 corn tortillas. Top each with a halibut piece and sprinkle with the fennel-coriander mixture. Garnish each with a spoonful of Grilled Lemon Aioli, Cucumber Pico de Gallo, and cilantro leaves.

GRILLED LEMON AIOLI

Heat a cast-iron pan over medium-high heat. Zest 1 lemon (to get about 2 teaspoons zest), and then cut it in half. Char the halves, cut-side down, on a hot cast-iron skillet or outdoor grill for 2 to 3 minutes. Don't overcook or the juice will dry up. Squeeze juice from the lemon halves and combine with 1 cup mayonnaise, 1½ roasted garlic cloves, and 1 teaspoon salt. Makes 1¼ cups.

CUCUMBER PICO DE GALLO

Combine 1 seeded and diced Fresno chile pepper, 1 seeded and diced jalapeño, ½ seeded and diced serrano pepper, 1 diced English cucumber, ½ of a diced red onion, the juice of 3 limes, and kosher salt to taste in a bowl. Makes about 3½ cups.

MADRE! OAXACAN RESTAURANT AND MEZCALERIA

1261 CABRILLO AVENUE #100
TORRANCE, CA 90501
310.974.8005
MADRERESTAURANTS.COM

The Torrance flagship of this Oaxacan restaurant is nondescript on the outside, but as richly appointed and vibrant inside as the food and drink served. Sink into a supple leather booth or barstool to enjoy a nibble or sip. Old-world Talavera ceramic tiles add a fiesta of color to the back of the bar and a bright geometry to the dining room walls that feels modern. A large mural labeled "La Jefa" (the boss) pays homage to chef and owner Ivan Vasquez's mother, Lucila Rodriguez, who taught him how to cook back home in Oaxaca. Floor-to-ceiling steel casement windows divide the space while maintaining an airy and inviting atmosphere. This is a place you want to stay awhile. One taste of the expertly executed Oaxacan cuisine and you're guaranteed to return. The exclamation mark at the end of the restaurant's name drives that home, but Chef Vasquez goes on to describe what is so special about his ancient native cuisine.

"Oaxaca is one of the states that preserves lot of pre-Hispanic culture and tradition. We have recipes from previous generations. Some villages don't even speak Spanish, but a different dialect. Oaxaca has its own cheese, peppers, and tortillas (*tlayudas*), and it's considered the land of the seven moles!" Vasquez enthuses.

At the bar, Beverage Director Bryant Orozco will happily suss out your likes and dislikes to deftly fuse tequila, mezcal, or an agave cousin—over four hundred bottles in all—with fresh California ingredients. He offers a handful of approachable mezcals he refers to as his "gateway mezcal" behind the bar, for the uninitiated. For whiskey or gin drinkers, bartenders will suggest a mezcal with complementary flavor notes. "I tend to save mezcal made in small batches or rarities for more experienced drinkers or the adventurous," Orozco admits.

Order a mezcal flight and the liquid journey comes with orange wedges and earthy *chapulines*, boiled and dried grasshoppers. Further fortify yourself on chorizo and potato-stuffed *molotes* (similar to empanadas but made with fresh masa), dig into a tower of tangy shrimp ceviche, or share a sampling of three of the traditional Oaxacan moles offered . . . just save room for the barbacoa de chivo, goat meat bathed in a complex guajillo chile paste and slow-cooked with avocado leaves and spices (page 30). If you have even a tiny bit of room left, order the mezcal flan to experience how this traditional Mexican spirit plays well in desserts.

EL CHAPO Y KATE SERVES 1

Beverage Director Bryant Orozco says that many patrons have begun asking for high-proof tequilas. "They tell me they are bored of the 40% bottlings (spoiled by mezcal, I assume!) and are looking for something with more of a kick, for more character." This cocktail is spiked with high-proof blanco tequila, and it exemplifies the bar's innovative approach to mixology. Here, prickly pear brandy mingles with cucumber, lime, and a hint of habanero in the bitters.

Tajín Rim Salt (*recipe follows*)

1 ounce Pueblo Viejo blanco tequila

1 ounce Ventura Spirits Opuntia prickly pear (cactus pear brandy)

1 ounce fresh Cucumber Water (*recipe follows*)

¾ ounce freshly squeezed lime juice

¾ ounce agave syrup (3 parts agave nectar to 1 part water)

2 dashes Scrappy's Firewater bitters

Cucumber ribbon

1   Rim a rocks glass with the rim salt. Fill the glass with ice.

2   Combine the tequila, Opuntia, Cucumber Water, lime juice, agave syrup, and bitters in an ice-filled shaker. Shake vigorously. Strain over the fresh ice in the glass. Garnish with cucumber ribbon.

TAJÍN RIM SALT

Combine equal parts Tajín seasoning and kosher salt, and store in an airtight container in a cool, dry place up to several months. Makes as much as you wish.

CUCUMBER WATER

Puree 1 English cucumber with skin in a blender. Fine-strain to remove solids. Store in a clean jar up to 2 days in the refrigerator. Makes about 1 cup.

WHAT'S IN A NAME?

"This cocktail has been on our menu since Madre! first opened. It was created by our then Beverage Consultant, Feisser Stone, and me. We made it when El Chapo was having his [reputed] romantic adventure with actress Kate del Castillo[1], so we used their names as inspiration. Chapo represents the spicy and sour flavors, while Kate represents the s weet and refreshing notes," says Chef Vasquez.

[1] Kate del Castillo has denied allegations of a romantic relationship with El Chapo.

MADRE! GOAT BARBACOA TACOS SERVES 10 TO 15

In Oaxaca, barbacoa is traditionally cooked over wood in agave leaf-lined pits, which creates a slow, moist heat. At Madre!, Chef Vasquez braises barbacoa (lamb is his favorite) on the stovetop, sometimes lining the pot with agave or banana leaves. Avocado leaves are used in cooking in southern parts of Mexico like Oaxaca for the flavor that they impart—a distinctive herbaceousness, with notes of anise and mint. "We also use avocado leaves for our black bean paste, menudo, and chicken barbacoa," Chef Vasquez offers. Toasting the dried leaves on a hot *comal*, or cast-iron skillet, for a few seconds on each side heightens the flavor. Dried avocado leaves are readily available at Latin markets. Substitute a few bay leaves and a sprinkling of anise seeds for a close approximation. If you prefer, substitute an equal weight of lamb for the goat in this recipe.

5 pounds goat leg meat

2 pounds goat rib meat

2 cups fresh lime juice

20 guajillo chiles

10 dried avocado leaves

15 garlic cloves, peeled

2 yellow onions, coarsely chopped

¼ cup white vinegar or apple cider vinegar

¾ cup dried Mexican oregano

¼ cup dried thyme

3 tablespoons salt

½ teaspoon cumin

3 cinnamon sticks

5 whole cloves

5 whole black peppercorns

30 yellow corn tortillas, warmed

Toppings: shredded cabbage, finely diced white onion, cilantro, tomatillo salsa, lime wedges

1 Place the meat in a large container filled with 1 gallon of cold water and the lime juice. Gently massage the meat in the liquid to "wash." Let soak 10 minutes. Drain and transfer the meat to a large Dutch oven or stockpot. Set aside.

2 Working in batches, lightly char the chiles, avocado leaves, and garlic on a searing hot griddle or cast-iron skillet on all sides.

3 Remove the stems and seeds from the chiles and soak them in ½ gallon of hot water for 45 minutes to soften. Combine the chiles, soaking water, 5 of the avocado leaves, the garlic cloves, onions, vinegar, oregano, thyme, salt, cumin, cinnamon sticks, cloves, and peppercorns in a blender and blend until smooth.

4 Pour the salsa over the meat. Add water as necessary to cover. Place the pot over medium heat and cook for 2½ hours or until the meat reaches an internal temperature of 160°F and is fall-apart tender. Add the remaining avocado leaves for the last 15 minutes of cooking.

5 Shred the cooked meat and spoon it onto warm tortillas. Top the meat with cabbage, onion, cilantro, and tomatillo salsa. Serve with lime wedges.

SALAZAR

2490 FLETCHER DRIVE
LOS ANGELES, CA 90039
SALAZARLA.COM

Chef Jonathan Aviles has taken what is arguably one of the hottest Mexican restaurants in Los Angeles to higher heights. Salazar—named for the former Salazar Mazda garage it is housed in—was launched in 2016 by restaurateur Andrew Silverman and street taco king Chef Esdras Ochoa, who has since taken his successful taco concept to Hong Kong. That departure allowed Aviles to move from his role as Chef de Cuisine to Executive Chef at this hip hangout by the LA River in Frogtown.

The retro-modern restaurant with its indoor-outdoor bar, open kitchen, and massive patio surrounded by soaring palms, arching shade trees, and towering saguaro cactus feels like you've come to the coolest backyard barbecue around. Quench your thirst with Beverage Director Adan Maldonado's mezcal-centric craft cocktails like the savory, briny, and completely refreshing Paradise Cove with seaweed, cucumber, mint, and lime. Tamer chugs include on-tap micheladas or juicy agua frescas like the tamarind one he shares on page 33.

Classically trained at Le Cordon Bleu, Chef Aviles started cooking traditional Mexican dishes at an early age by his grandmother's side while growing up in Pasadena. A pastime he shares today with his own kids—eleven-year-old Rudiger and five-year-old Riot Rose. Chef Aviles's Hispanic roots, classical training, and stints in an array of restaurants sharpened his craft and have allowed him to bring the techniques and flavors from other culinary traditions into his cooking at Salazar in delicious ways. While you won't find in-your-face global fusion mash-ups on the menu, you will find his innovative approach to Sonoran-style barbecued dishes cooked over mesquite and oak. The carne asada tacos are the customer taco favorite by far (something Aviles attributes to diner familiarity), but he admits he is most inspired to get creative with whatever the seasons bring to the kitchen door.

Cauliflower is one of his favorite vegetables, and the taco recipe he shares on page 34 will make it yours, too. By happenstance, it's a completely vegan taco, but you won't miss the protein, salsa, cheese, or crema when you bite into meaty cauliflower flavored with wisps of woodsmoke and char, topped with sweet fennel and sour-pickled wild onions. It hits every expected note and so many unexpected ones, which is exactly what great cooking does.

SPIKED TAMARIND AGUA FRESCA
SERVES 8 TO 10 (MAKES ABOUT 1 GALLON)

At Salazar, they make tamarind paste by cooking the flesh of tamarind pods with sugar. You can find packages of pods at most Latin grocery stores. Or, for a quicker avenue to quench your thirst, substitute jarred tamarind puree, sweetened and diluted to taste.

1 (16-ounce) package tamarind pods (about 24 pods)

¾ teaspoon kosher salt

1 cup granulated sugar

1 gallon water

Sugar to taste

2 ounces blanco tequila

Orchid blossom

1 Peel and devein the tamarind pods. Combine the tamarind, salt, sugar, and 1 quart of the water in a large saucepan.

2 Bring the mixture to a boil, and then reduce the heat to a simmer. Cook for 10 minutes. Set aside to soak for 10 minutes.

3 Roll up your sleeves and, with clean hands, remove the seeds from the soft tamarind pulp, and discard. Blend the pulp with the warm water. Pour the blended mixture through a fine-mesh strainer into a gallon-size container. Stir in 3 quarts of cold water. Refrigerate and serve chilled.

4 Add the blanco tequila to a Collins glass. Fill the glass with ice. Top with the Tamarind Agua Fresca and stir with a bar spoon. Garnish with a fresh orchid blossom.

CAULIFLOWER TACOS WITH FENNEL & RAMPS SERVES 4

Salazar Executive Chef Jonathan Aviles has created a vegan taco that is refined, flavorful, and satisfying. A trio of aromatic bulbs—ramp, fennel, and leek—add delicious complexity to meaty grilled cauliflower. Ramps are a wild onion with a fleeting season. Pickle them when available in the spring, or find them pickled in jars at fine grocers. I purchased a jar of Blackberry Farm Pickled Ramps online, made from ramps foraged all the way across the country from Salazar, in the mountains of Tennessee.

2 heads cauliflower

3 tablespoons olive oil

Kosher salt and freshly ground black pepper

1 leek

2 fennel bulbs

Corn or flour tortillas

Coarsely chopped Pickled Ramps (*recipe follows*)

Cilantro leaves

1 Prepare a fire in an outdoor grill.

2 Cut the cauliflower into 1-inch "steaks." Rub all over with 2 tablespoons of the olive oil. Season lightly with salt and pepper. Grill until lightly charred but firm. Remove and let cool. Cut into bite-size pieces. Set aside.

3 Cut away the green top from the leek. Quarter the white bulb lengthwise. Cut the bulb crosswise into ½-inch pieces. Place in a bowl of water to rinse off excess dirt. Drain and set aside.

4 Remove the stems from the fennel bulbs (reserve the fronds for garnish, if desired). Halve lengthwise, remove the core, slice, and set aside.

5 Heat the remaining oil in a sauté pan over medium-high heat. Add the leeks and sauté until just translucent. Season lightly. Add the fennel and cook until just tender. Add the grilled cauliflower pieces and season again lightly with salt and pepper to taste.

6 Place the vegetable mixture in a tortilla, top with pickled ramps, cilantro, and reserved fennel fronds, if desired. Serve warm.

PICKLED RAMPS

Place 2 cups ramp bulbs of uniform size in a sterile jar or nonreactive container. Place ¼ cup each of pickling spice, sugar, and kosher salt with 1 quart each of water and white vinegar in a saucepan and bring to a boil over high heat. Carefully strain, if desired, or pour the hot pickling liquid over the ramps. Seal the jar with a tight-fitting lid, or with its lid or plastic wrap. Refrigerate. Makes 1 quart.

MOSTO & TACOLICIOUS

741 VALENCIA STREET
SAN FRANCISCO, CA 94110
415.649.6077
MOSTOBAR.COM
TACOLICIOUS.COM

Once upon a time in the City by the Bay, a girl fluttered into a hip Spanish restaurant called Laïola, the Spanish word for butterfly. Sara Deseran was the food editor for a slick city magazine (and full disclosure: my dear friend). As occupation would have it, she soon was conversing with the owner, Joe Hargrave, and welcome sparks flew. She became a regular because she loved the food and was beginning to love the guy, too. This was just before the Great Recession, and Bay Area restaurants were feeling it no matter how well-stocked the bar, how crispy the chickpea croquettes, or how addictive the chorizo-stuffed dates.

Though Laïola eventually closed, their new marriage and a world of possibilities bloomed. On a needed escape to Mexico City, the two found inspiration everywhere they ate. They sipped tequila and mezcal, nibbled on steak tacos at upscale El Califa, and swooned over the buttery ahi tuna tostadas at acclaimed Contramar. They could not get their fill. When they returned to the Golden State, they craved the food they'd left behind. It was Mexican food that the burrito-centric taquerias of San Francisco just didn't offer, served with the easy, sit-down sophistication of a full-service restaurant.

Before their trip, Joe had agreed to open a food stall at the new Thursday farmers' market at San Francisco's Ferry Building. It was assumed he'd be slinging Spanish fare, but to the market director's surprise, Joe said that he'd be selling tacos—specifically, braised-meat *tacos guisado* like guajillo-bathed short ribs served with sides of grilled corn slathered in recado, an achiote-and-spice paste. The stand was so popular that Joe and Sara were soon brainstorming a full-service Tacolicious restaurant in the old Laïola space.

Fast-forward and the Tacolicious train is chugging along at its brick-and-mortar flagship in the Marina District and on Valencia Street in the Mission District, but also at locations in North Beach, Palo Alto, and San Jose. That first little taco stand that proved they could, is still going strong at the Ferry Building. Renamed Tacolicious Chico, it's a quick-service spot that keeps the focus on tacos guisados. Tacolicious has spawned other concepts like Mosto, the tequila and mezcal bar next door to the Mission District location, and an international extension called Taco Lab by Tacolicious, in the stunning San Miguel de Allende, Mexico. Next stop? Best to stay tuned . . .

MOSTO'S CANTARITO PRIMAVERA SERVES 1

Cantaritos are Jalisco-rooted cocktails similar to a Paloma, and this Cantarito is Mosto's ode to spring. Bartenders use top-quality El Silencio mezcal and Whalebird Dry Hopped Pamplemousse kombucha for a float with a dryer finish. If you like things a bit sweeter, top with Squirt, a favorite soft drink in Mexico and a more traditional finish. Cantaritos are named for the clay cup that they are traditionally served in, but a Collins glass will do.

- 1½ ounce Strawberry-Infused Mezcal (recipe follows)
- ¾ ounce Lo-Fi Gentian Amaro
- ½ ounce agave syrup
- Juice of half a lime
- Juice of half a lemon
- Juice of half a grapefruit
- Pinch of salt
- Kombucha of your choice to float
- Garnish: pineapple leaf, lemon wheel, lime wheel, and strawberry

Place everything into a shaker with ice. Shake and strain into a glass or cantarito filled with ice. Top with a float of kombucha—slowly pour the fermented drink over the back of a spoon so that it creates a thin layer of liquid to top off the cocktail. Garnish with a pineapple leaf, lemon wheel, lime wheel, and ½ strawberry.

STRAWBERRY-INFUSED MEZCAL

Stem and quarter 1 pint of fresh strawberries and slice the berries into smaller pieces. Combine the sliced strawberries with a 750-milliliter bottle of good-quality mezcal. Let sit at room temperature for 24 hours. Strain. Makes 1 (750-ml) bottle.

Tacolicious turns to Pete's Meats in San Francisco for the locally made pastrami in this taco, but substitute the best you can find near you.

CARAWAY DRESSING

¼ cup apple cider vinegar

2 teaspoons Dijon mustard

1 tablespoon caraway seeds, toasted

1 teaspoon kosher salt

1 tablespoon honey

¼ cup grapeseed oil

MUSTARD-MANZANA AIOLI

1 teaspoon canola oil

2 tablespoons diced Granny Smith apple

½ cup good-quality mayonnaise

2 tablespoons whole-grain mustard

2 minced chipotles in adobo sauce

1 teaspoon kosher salt

2 cups finely shredded red and green cabbage

1 pound of pastrami, sliced ¼-inch thick

6 flour tortillas

Toppings: diced white onion and chopped fresh cilantro

1   Make the dressing by mixing the vinegar, mustard, caraway, salt, and honey in a blender. Slowly add the oil through the hole in the lid until the dressing is emulsified and creamy. Toss the cabbage with the dressing and set aside to marinate 15 minutes.

2   Make the aioli by sautéing the apple in the oil over medium heat until soft. Place the apple, mayonnaise, mustard, chipotle, and salt in a food processor fitted with the metal blade and process until smooth.

3   Sear the pastrami slices in a heavy skillet until heated through and lightly caramelized.

4   Heat a tortilla on a hot, dry skillet until lightly toasted and puffed. Spread a bit of the Mustard-Manzana Aioli on the hot tortilla and top with pastrami, slaw, white onion, and cilantro. Serve warm.

JAPANESE NORI TACO

The sushi taco is trending. This global mash-up of cuisines exemplifies the tacos-without-borders craze that has taken hold in every corner of the country—whether it's fillings enveloped by Indian Paratha Dough (page 110), folded in spongy Ethiopian Injera Bread (page 85), or cradled in a crisp cookie shell as a dessert taco (page 155)—the taco has been translated into countless cuisines.

The chef of Norigami Tacos, a pop-up in Southern California, claims to have created the East Asian riff on Mexican street food, while others aren't so quick to relinquish credit. An ocean away, Okinawa's Charlie's Tacos opened in the 1950s, serving Mexican-style taco fillings like ground beef, shredded lettuce, tomato, and cheese in fried rice-paper shells, as well as bowls of the Okinawan taco-donburi hybrid called "taco rice." For half a dozen years, Wasabi Juan's in Birmingham, Alabama, has been rolling tacos and burritos stuffed with sushi fillings and crunchy road trip snacks like spicy Dorito crumbs and tortilla chip crispies swaddled in soy wrappers and nori. And inside Boston's Time Out Market, Gogo Ya serves crunchy, battered nori tacos stuffed with fine-dining finesse—torched hamachi with truffled jalapeño butter and scallions or Maine lobster with tamari butter glaze and sake–sea urchin sauce. No matter the shell, how you fill it, or where you eat it, the taco is universal.

SALMON POKE NORI TACOS SERVES 2 TO 3

In these tacos, nori—the sheets of dried seaweed that more often wraps rings of sticky rice for sushi—gets a tempura treatment. Draping the just-fried sheets over an aluminum foil mold to cool allows the pliable wrapper to firm up like a taco shell ready for filling. The raw fish filling is inspired by Hawaiian poke, which means "to slice" in the island's native tongue. Poke originated as a simple dish of sliced, fresh Hawaiian reef fish eaten by locals, but morphed into a donburi-style rice bowl topped with slices of raw ahi tuna to cater to the preferences of the Japanese workers who flooded the island in the 1800s. Like the Mexican taco, today's "mainland" poke bowls bear little resemblance to the original sliced fish dish or Japanese-influenced bowls of Hawaiian poke. Nowadays, whether you're a purist or a rule breaker, you can choose from a smorgasbord of fillings, garnishes, and sauces, and even stuff it all in a tempura-fried nori shell and call it a "taco."

¾ pound skinless sushi-grade salmon fillet

¼ cup soy sauce

1 teaspoon sesame oil

1 teaspoon unseasoned rice vinegar

1 tablespoon of black or white sesame seeds, or a combination

FRIED NORI TACO SHELLS

1 quart vegetable oil, for frying

1¼ cups rice flour

½ teaspoon salt

1 egg yolk

1 cup ice water

6 sheets of dried nori seaweed, cut into 6-inch rounds

Toppings: Pickled Radishes (*recipe follows*), sliced green onions, diced avocado, sriracha sauce, Japanese mayonnaise, and sliced shiso leaves (optional)

1 Dice the salmon into ½-inch cubes. Mix the diced salmon with the soy sauce, sesame oil, unseasoned rice vinegar, and sesame seeds in a mixing bowl. (Chill until you are ready to assemble the tacos.)

2 Crumble up a large piece of aluminum foil to create a mold to drape the fried nori over to create a shell. Heat the oil in a deep, heavy skillet over medium heat until it reaches 375°F.

3 While the oil is heating, make the tempura batter by whisking the rice flour, salt, egg yolk, and ice water together in a mixing bowl until no lumps remain.

4 Submerge the nori rounds in the tempura batter to cover. Transfer one battered round of nori into the hot oil using tongs, and drop the round away from you. Fry 1 to 2 minutes per side, until light and crispy.

5 Remove the nori from the oil and while it is still hot and pliable, drape it over the foil mold to form a taco-shell shape. Once formed, transfer to a rack to cool completely while you fry the remaining nori.

6 Divide the salmon mixture among 6 Nori Taco Shells. Top with Pickled Radish slices, green onions, and avocado. Drizzle with a bit of sriracha, Japanese mayonnaise, and shiso leaves.

PICKLED RADISHES

Combine 4 thinly sliced radishes, 4 tablespoons
unseasoned rice vinegar, 1 teaspoon sugar,
and a pinch of kosher salt in a bowl and stir to
combine. Cover and refrigerate for 30 minutes,
or up to 12 hours. Makes ½ cup.

TAQUERIA 27

1615 S. FOOTHILL DRIVE
SALT LAKE CITY, UT 84108
385.259.0712
TAQUERIA27.COM

In the Foothills neighborhood of Salt Lake City, Chef Todd Gardiner and his wife, Kristin, opened their first Taqueria 27 back in 2012. Todd loved the flavors and ingredients of Mexico and felt that tacos were "a perfect way to get delicious food in the mouth." The 27 in the restaurant name refers to the Gardiner family's lucky number—the day of the month that both the chef and his daughter were born. It appears that luck continues to pay off, as Taqueria 27 has grown to five locations.

Chef Gardiner's artisan approach to the taco is informed by his classic culinary training and many years in the restaurant business. "Inspiration comes from the simple fact I can mix and match techniques and flavors and put that in a corn or flour tortilla." He also believes that tacos are made for sharing, and dining out shouldn't be stuffy, so he made Taqueria 27 a place people could have fun while enjoying a communal meal.

Every day at Taqueria 27 brings a new taco special like Tacos Alambre (Wagyu beef, pork belly, Oaxaca cheese, and salsa verde), T27 Fried Shrimp Taco (crispy crustaceans, cucumber-jicama slaw, and spicy pineapple salsa), or the Buffalo Chicken Taco (spicy chicken, carrot-celery slaw, green chile–gorgonzola, and dainty greens). Surprisingly, Gardiner admits that his customers love any featured taco with mashed potatoes in it.

It is obvious that he and his team have fun brainstorming creative new takes on the taco, but they make no apologies for bucking tradition, because the food they serve draws crowds and garners fervent fans. That is not to say that they don't respect the classics or draw upon timeless techniques for making asada, carnitas, and barbacoa. They just apply those techniques in fresh new ways.

You'll find a rotating roundup of dish-of-the-day specials: M.O.D. (margarita), T.O.D (taco), G.O.D (guacamole), F.O.D (fish), and D.O.D (dessert). These fleeting dishes are a fun way to capture attention and entice, while menu mainstays like Duck Confit tacos, Angus Carne Asada (page 47), and Achiote Marinated Grilled Chicken Breast turn customers into restaurant regulars.

Though this is Mormon country, the bar boasts close to forty bottles of 100% agave tequila and mezcal, and a dozen tequila cocktails including the T27 Grand Rouge (page 46), which Gardiner considers the "perfect gateway cocktail." It's a Herradura Silver margarita with a rosy float of Malbec. It's also the perfect cocktail to sip with his Angus Carne Asada Tacos with Grilled Cactus (page 47).

T27 GRAND ROUGE   SERVES 1

Chef Gardiner suggests a full-bodied red like a robust Argentinian Malbec as the float to top the restaurant's top-shelf margarita, a drink created by former restaurant manager Josh Jones. Gardiner believes agave spirits have taken off "because once folks try a fine 100% agave tequila, they appreciate the craft that goes into making it. Good tequila is also very easy to use in a variety of cocktails that traditionally use other spirits."

1 ounce freshly squeezed lime juice

½ ounce freshly squeezed orange juice

1 tablespoon agave syrup

1 ounce 100% agave silver tequila

Orange wheel

1 ounce red wine, preferably Malbec

½ ounce Grand Marnier

Combine the juices, agave syrup, and tequila in an ice-filled shaker tin. Shake vigorously. Strain into a 12-ounce rocks glass. Carefully place an orange wheel on the surface of the cocktail and then "float" the red wine and Grand Marnier on top of the orange wheel to create a layered effect.

ANGUS CARNE ASADA
TACOS WITH GRILLED CACTUS SERVES 4

Slightly charred, tender grilled beef is a taco favorite. Traditionally made from cuts of beef that come from the plate or skirt, hanger, or flank, Chef Gardiner also uses chuck tail-flap, which comes from the short rib of the chuck and is loaded with rich, beefy flavor.

**BALSAMIC
CHIMICHURRI**

1½ bunches flat-leaf parsley (about 3 cups leaves)

1 bunch cilantro (about 2 cups leaves)

¾ cup olive oil

1 tablespoon balsamic vinegar

½ tablespoon kosher salt

1 teaspoon black pepper

1 pound Angus inside skirt steak or chuck tail-flap

8 (6-inch) corn or flour tortillas

1 to 2 ounces shredded lettuce

Grilled Cactus and Avocado Salsa (*recipe follows*)

1 Place all the chimichurri ingredients in a blender. Blend until smooth.

2 Marinate the meat in ¼ cup of the chimichurri for up to 24 hours. Reserve the remaining chimichurri for serving.

3 Prepare a fire in an outdoor grill or heat a cast-iron skillet for several minutes over high heat. Grill over direct heat or sear the beef for 2 minutes per side for rare, or to desired doneness. Remove the meat and let it rest 4 to 5 minutes. Dice it into small pieces.

4 Warm the tortillas. Divide the lettuce, meat, and salsa among the tortillas. Drizzle the toppings with a bit of the chimichurri. Serve warm.

GRILLED CACTUS AND AVOCADO SALSA   MAKES 1¼ CUPS

1 medium-size cactus paddle (thorns removed)

1 lime

½ cup prepared Pico de Gallo (see page 89)

1 ripe avocado, peeled and cut into ¼-inch dice

Kosher salt and freshly ground black pepper

1 Prepare a fire in an outdoor grill.

2 Place the cactus paddle over direct heat for about 2 minutes per side to develop charred grill marks. Remove and let cool slightly. Carefully, cut into ¼-inch cubes.

3 Toss the diced cactus in a mixing bowl with the freshly squeezed juice of the lime. Add the Pico de Gallo and avocado and toss to combine. Season to taste with the salt and pepper.

THE TEQUILA DAISY SERVES 1

The Daisy is a venerable "mother cocktail" in the sour category from which countless bright cocktails are spawned. It is comprised of a base spirit and liqueur, citrus juice, and sometimes a syrup to sweeten or seltzer to lengthen. Gin is the spirit base of the OG Daisy, but variations like the vodka Cosmo or brandy Sidecar, are aplenty.

Perhaps the most popular spin on the Daisy is the tequila-spiked margarita—the Spanish word for daisy—which blossomed to popularity during Prohibition days when people ventured across the border to slake their thirsts for spirited refreshment. Origin stories about its creation abound and are impossible to verify, but its ingredients remain steadfast. Whether served neat, on the rocks, frozen, with salted rim or without, this classic tequila sour endures.

2 ounces blanco tequila

1 ounce Cointreau

1 ounce lime juice

½ ounce simple syrup (optional)

Lime wheel and zest curl

Combine all the ingredients in an ice-filled shaker tin. Shake vigorously. Strain into a martini glass or coupe and serve neat, or strain into an ice-filled rocks or margarita glass, with or without a salted rim. Serve with a lime wheel and zest curl.

CRIOLLO LATIN KITCHEN

16 N. SAN FRANCISCO STREET
FLAGSTAFF, AZ 86001
928.774.0541
CRIOLLOLATINKITCHEN.COM

In a converted movie theater in historic downtown Flagstaff, Criollo prides itself on showcasing the local and sustainable ingredients it sources from farmers and ranchers in the surrounding high mountain area—a philosophy that extends well beyond the menu. Kitchen scraps are composted, a percentage of sales goes to fund microloans for farmers, and the rustic planks that line the walls are from local beetle-killed Ponderosa pine trees.

Criollo deserves high marks for those endeavors alone, but one taste of the food—beer-battered catfish, pork belly bathed in fermented black garlic mojo, or guajillo-marinated layers of pork served with charred pineapple in Tacos Al Pastor (page 54)—and you realize that this place hits on all cylinders. Chef David Smith's experiences in other kitchens distilled his approach to cooking. "I learned how to make black garlic from Nick Balla and Courtney Burns of the former Bar Tartine. Their black garlic potatoes are one of the best dishes I've had. I used the same concept of matching black garlic with a fatty element and then something spicy and acidic to balance the flavor." His dishes are all about building flavorful complexity as his elevated Zesty Crema and Pickled Onions in the Al Pastor recipe exemplify.

Criollo is a second venture for Paul and Laura Moir, who also own Brix, a nationally recognized white tablecloth restaurant on the edge of downtown. Growing up, Laura traveled throughout Mexico and Central America in a converted school bus with her family, while Paul grew up regularly vacationing there. So opening a Latin restaurant spoke to a shared passion. Criollo refers to one of Latin heritage born in the Americas. In the case of the restaurant, it's about merging Mexican classics with local ingredients.

Stop in at Criollo any weekday from 3:00 to 6:00 p.m. for happy hour to get a sense of what the Flagstaff community is like. You'll find ultrarunners and skiers next to college kids and artists, families and empty nesters. It's a laid-back melting pot of demographics converging to share great food and drink—two-buck Tecates, sixty-four-ounce mason jar margaritas spiked with your choice of any of the forty-five agave spirits offered, or great wines paired with family-style platters of snacks like crispy plantains, chicharrón, chipotle-lime peanuts, wings, or any of a half dozen different tacos. It's a scene that is completely local and by all accounts deliciously sustainable.

TOO MATCHA TEQUILA

SERVES 1

The name says it all, so why not order up a synergistic cocktail that tempers tequila with a dose of the eye-opening caffeine and antioxidants that green tea provides. It certainly beats Red Bull and anything.

1½ ounces Milagro reposado tequila

½ ounce fresh lime juice

½ ounce pineapple juice (fresh is best)

½ ounces Jalapeño Syrup (*recipe follows*)

1 teaspoon matcha powder

Lime wheel

Mint sprig

Combine the tequila, lime juice, pineapple juice, Jalapeño Syrup, and matcha powder in an ice-filled shaker tin. Shake vigorously. Strain over fresh ice in a rocks glass. Garnish with a lime wheel and mint sprig.

JALAPEÑO SYRUP

Blend 1 cup agave syrup, 1 cup water, 1 to 2 roughly chopped jalapeños, ¼ roughly chopped pasilla chile, and ½ serrano (if you like extra heat) in a high-speed blender. Strain into a clean pint jar. Store in the refrigerator up to 1 month. Makes 1 pint.

AL PASTOR TACOS WITH ZESTY CREMA, ROASTED PINEAPPLE, AND PICKLED ONIONS

SERVES 4 TO 6

The pork needs to be sliced very thin before it is marinated, so be sure your knives are sharp. It's helpful to put the meat in the freezer for about 45 minutes to firm up for easier slicing. This loaf-pan method for cooking the meat is a great way to replicate the layers that you get when spit-roasted meats are sliced off the *trompo* in Mexico. Just know that the meat shrinks down considerably as it cooks and the fat renders. Marinate the meat at least 8 hours before you cook it. You can even cook it a day before you plan to serve it. Just slice and reheat the meat in a skillet with a bit of the reserved marinade as you assemble the tacos.

AL PASTOR MARINADE

8 guajillo chiles, stemmed and deseeded

¾ cup pineapple juice

½ cup orange juice

4 tablespoons lemon juice

4 tablespoons lime juice

1 teaspoon chipotle powder

4 tablespoons brown sugar

4 tablespoons chopped garlic

4 tablespoons ground cumin

½ teaspoon ground cloves

1 tablespoon dried Mexican oregano

2 tablespoons kosher salt

2 pounds pork shoulder, thinly sliced

15 corn tortillas, warmed

Toppings: Zesty Crema (*recipe follows*), Roasted Pineapple (*recipe follows*), Pickled Onions (*recipe follows*), and chopped fresh cilantro

1. Preheat the oven to 300°F. Toast the chiles on a baking sheet just until you smell the aroma of the peppers, 1 to 2 minutes. As soon as you smell them, count to 15 and then remove the pan from the oven.

2. Soak the toasted chiles in very hot water for 15 to 20 minutes until soft. Drain and place the chiles in a blender with the remaining marinade ingredients; blend until the marinade is very smooth.

3. Place the pork in a large mixing bowl. Pour the marinade over the meat, reserving ¼ cup for later use, should you need to reheat the meat before assembling the tacos. Toss the meat to coat it well.

4. Stack the marinade-coated pork slices in an overlapping fashion in a nonstick loaf pan. Cover the loaf pan with plastic wrap. Marinate the meat at least 8 hours or up to 24 hours in the refrigerator.

5. Preheat the oven to 275°F. Cover the plastic-covered loaf pan with a piece of aluminum foil (the plastic helps retain moisture and is safe in the oven at this temperature). Bake until the middle layers of meat reach an internal temperature of 190°F when tested with a meat thermometer, about 4 hours. Let the pork rest and cool. Remove the loaf of meat from the pan and slice it across the layers as you would slice a loaf of bread.

6 Build the tacos by spreading a dollop of the Zesty Crema on a warm tortilla. Top with hot sliced pork (reheat the pork in a sauté pan with a bit of the reserved marinade if needed). Arrange a spoonful of pineapple on top of the meat. Finish with a sprinkling of Pickled Onion and chopped cilantro.

ZESTY CREMA

Combine 2 cups sour cream, 1 bunch roughly chopped cilantro, 1 seeded and finely chopped jalapeño, roughly chopped chipotle chiles from ¼ of a (7½-ounce) can, the juice and grated zest of 1 lime, and 1 tablespoon kosher salt in a mixing bowl. Mix well. Makes about 2 cups.

ROASTED PINEAPPLE

Preheat the oven to 425°F. Remove the top, base, and skin from 1 pineapple so that no brown spots remain. Slice it lengthwise into ½-inch planks with core intact. Coat the pieces lightly with canola oil and arrange in a single layer on a parchment-lined baking sheet. Roast for 15 minutes or until nicely caramelized. Remove and let the pineapple cool. Cut away and discard the core. Cut the fruit into ¼-inch cubes. Makes about 3 cups.

PICKLED ONIONS

Toss 1 finely diced white onion in a mixing bowl with the grated zest and juice of 3 limes and 1 tablespoon kosher salt. Set aside for 1 hour, stirring often. Makes about 1 cup.

TOMASITA'S

500 S. GUADALUPE STREET
SANTA FE, NM 87501
505.983.5721
TOMASITAS.COM

Tomasita's is a Greek-owned Santa Fe institution that has been serving traditional northern New Mexican fare for almost half a century. It began with a stop for a quick bite at a hole-in-the-wall adobe café on Hickox Street by a young Georgia Maryol one serendipitous day in the early '70s. That bite transported her to her childhood in the Atrisco barrio of Albuquerque, where her Greek family lived next to Hispanic families with deep New Mexico roots. She loved the New Mexican food served at her friends' houses—the chile sauces, pork stews, and fresh tortillas. She was so inspired by her meal that she bought the café. Thankfully, cook Tomasita Leyba stayed put. Tomasita's recipes provided the magic that made what became her namesake restaurant a Santa Fe icon with a dedicated clientele. The restaurant eventually moved to a bigger location—the old territorial-style adobe train station on Gaudalupe Street—and a second location in Albuquerque recently opened.

After years working for non-profits in the San Francisco Bay Area, Georgia's son, George Gundrey, returned home and eventually took over the reins of Tomasita's. He subtly refined the menu by sourcing only the best quality products and local ingredients he could find to elevate the tried-and-true dishes that patrons expect and love. Specialties like the stuffed and smothered sopaipilla, a fried bread leavened with baking powder that puffs up like a pillow, which has become a favorite. Unlike a Tex-Mex puffy taco made from masa, New Mexican sopaipillas are made from wheat flour. The fried pockets are stuffed with savory fillings like ground beef, chicken, or cheese, and then smothered in red or green chile . . . or a mix of the two, which is referred to as "Christmas." Sopaipillas can also be ordered as bread for the table, served with honey in squeeze bottles, or dusted with cinnamon-sugar for dessert.

Favorite refreshments at Tomasita's include the huge frozen margaritas swirled with sangria, the house Gold Coin Margarita made with the restaurant's own añejo tequila, produced by Patrón. For something a bit more unusual, order up a Horny Juanita (page 57), created at Atrisco Cafe & Bar, Tomasita's restaurant sibling in Santa Fe that is named for that barrio where Georgia grew up. Made with reposado tequila and infused with raspberry puree and a splash of Chambord, the drink is definitely not your run-of-the-mill margarita.

HORNY JUANITA   SERVES 1

A splash of Chambord, a French black-raspberry liqueur, heightens the berry flavor of this blushing daisy cocktail.

2 ounces raspberries or raspberry puree

2 ounces fresh lemon juice

1 ounce simple syrup or agave syrup

1½ ounces Sauza Hornitos tequila

½ ounce Chambord

Lime wedge

If using fresh or frozen raspberries, blend or mash the raspberries thoroughly. Combine all the ingredients in a shaker with ice. Shake and strain into a sugar-rimmed martini glass. (Some raspberry pieces should come through the strainer.) Garnish with a lime wedge.

※

WHAT'S IN A NAME?

This cocktail's tongue-in-cheek name is a mash-up that references the brand of tequila used—Hornitos—and a patron-favorite waitress named Mary Jane.

TOMASITA'S STUFFED SOPAIPILLAS SERVES 8

Sopaipillas are said to have been invented in Albuquerque, New Mexico, two centuries ago. Usually drizzled with honey, the fry bread at Tomasita's can be ordered stuffed with savory fillings like ground beef and smothered in red, green, or "Christmas" (a mix of both) chile sauce. Dried red New Mexico chiles are readily available year-round, while roasted and chopped green chiles can be found in the freezer section of most grocery stores. During roasting season in New Mexico, you can purchase whole, freshly roasted green chiles. If you do, be sure to remove the stems and skins from the chiles before chopping.

SOPAIPILLAS

5 cups all-purpose flour

2 teaspoons salt

1 tablespoon baking powder

2 teaspoons vegetable shortening

1½ to 2 cups water

1 quart cooking oil

1 teaspoon olive oil

2 pounds ground beef

1½ teaspoons granulated garlic

1 tablespoon paprika

1½ teaspoons onion salt

4 cups Red or Green Chile Sauce, or a "Christmas" combo (recipe follows)

Toppings: shredded Monterey Jack cheese, shredded lettuce, diced tomato, and chopped white onion

1 Heat the oil in a skillet over medium-high heat. Add the beef and cook for 8 minutes or until cooked through, stirring to crumble. Drain the grease from the pan. Add the granulated garlic, paprika, onion salt, and tomato sauce, stirring to combine. Keep warm.

2 Mix all the dry Sopaipilla ingredients in a mixing bowl. Mix in the shortening well. Slowly add 1½ cups of the water and knead, adding more water as necessary, until a smooth dough forms.

3 Roll out the dough about ⅛-inch thick. Cut the dough into 32 3-inch squares or triangles of dough.

4 Heat the oil in a large pot to 375°F. Carefully drop 1 to 2 dough squares into the oil and gently spoon oil over the tops of the dough to make the dough puff up. Cook until golden brown, puffy, and crisp, 1 to 2 minutes.

5 Slit one side of each sopaipilla without going all the way through to create a pocket. Spoon the beef mixture inside the sopaipillas. Top with Red or Green Chile Sauce, or a mixture of the two, cheese, lettuce, tomato, and onion.

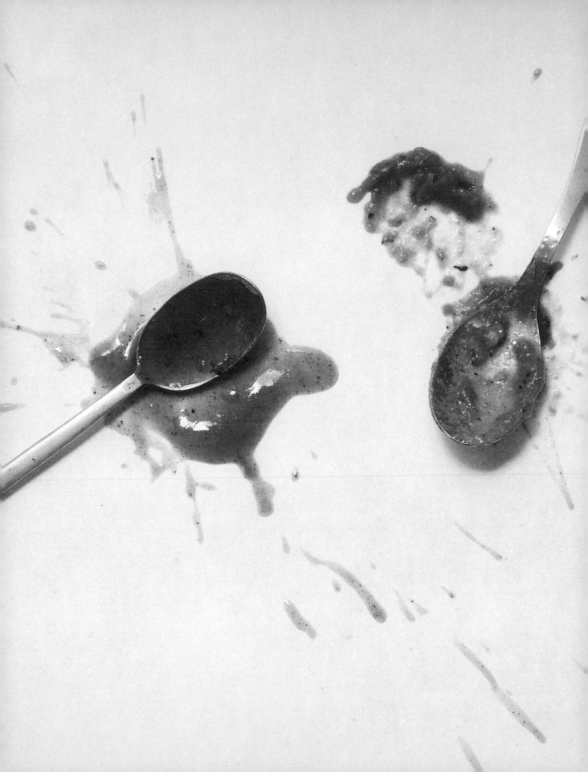

½ pound dried whole New Mexico red chiles or 1⅔ pounds fresh or thawed roasted and finely chopped New Mexico green chiles

2 tablespoons olive oil

2 tablespoons all-purpose flour

1½ teaspoons kosher salt

2 small garlic cloves, crushed (or 1½ teaspoons granulated garlic)

1   For the Red Chile Sauce, break off the stems and empty the seeds from each pod. Rinse the pods under running water, and then let them soak in a large bowl with boiling water to cover for 1 hour to soften. Drain the red chiles, discarding the soaking water. Place the pods in a blender and tamp them down. Add water just to the top of the chiles (about 3 cups). Blend on high speed to form a paste. (This paste can be frozen in small batches at this point for later use.) Put the paste in a large saucepan and heat it over medium-low heat. For Green Chile Sauce, place the chopped green chiles in a large saucepan and heat over medium-low heat.

2   Heat the oil in a small saucepan over medium-high heat. Whisk in the flour, stirring constantly, to avoid burning. Remove the pan from the heat when the roux is a deep nutty brown.

3   Slowly whisk the roux into the saucepan heating the red or green chiles, a little at a time, to thicken to a gravy-like consistency. You may not need all the roux. (If the chile sauce gets too thick, add water to thin as needed.) Stir in the salt and garlic.

4   Simmer on low heat for 20 minutes, stirring regularly. Do not boil, as that may burn the flour in the roux. Remove from the heat and adjust the salt and garlic to taste. Use the sauce in your recipe or store in the refrigerator for 3 to 4 days.

THE RESTAURANTS

MI MADRE'S RESTAURANT

2201 MANOR ROAD
AUSTIN, TX 78722
512.322.9721
MIMADRESRESTAURANT.COM

Breakfast tacos and Austin have been a thing for as long as I can remember. While in college in Texas, I often traveled with friends to the capital city, where cheesy scrambled eggs rolled in a freshly griddled flour tortilla were a mandatory start to the day. Whether it was whisked and wrapped by a friend's mom, plated with a puff of curly parsley and fruit at brunch someplace, or devoured out of hand at a taco stand, it was always delicious. Start with great ingredients—handmade flour tortillas, farm eggs, and lots of freshly grated cheese—and it's tough to mess up the breakfast taco. Though once in a while, all the key components, flavors, and textures come together in a way that sets a taco apart in its crowded category, and it's so delicious that it keeps you coming back again.

That's how Mi Madre's Restaurant has enticed bleary-eyed Austinites to rise and shine for decades. Simple as it is, their #0 with bacon, egg, potato, and cheese is the most-ordered on the menu, though the #8—vegetarian migas, the Tex-Mex specialty of eggs scrambled with pico de gallo, cheese, and tortilla chips that is a quick riff on Mexican chilaquiles—is right behind.

After moving from Saltillo, Mexico, back to his native Texas, Aurelio Torres and his wife, Rosa, opened Mi Madre's in 1990 near the UT campus with only a few hundred bucks in the bank. What started as a takeout taco shop became so popular, they soon expanded the dining room and patio. Thirty years later, the crowds haven't diminished, and seventy-year-old Aurelio works as hard as ever because he loves it. The Torres's son and daughter-in-law, who met at the Culinary Institute of America in New York, have joined the family business, adding the rooftop Techo Mezcaleria & Agave Bar above the dining room and a gastropub a few doors down. What started as a humble taco stand has grown into an East Austin casual dining empire with a staunch following that remains truly a family affair.

CAFÉ DE OLLA BORACHO SERVES 12

Mi Madre's house coffee—Texas Coffee Traders coffee—is brewed with piloncillo (Mexican cones of brown sugar), cinnamon, and Mexican chocolate seasoned with spices. You can swap a star anise pod or two for the anise seeds and cloves in the carafe, if desired.

½ cup piloncillo or brown sugar

3 (3-inch) cinnamon sticks

½ Abuela Mexican chocolate tablet

Pinch anise seeds

Pinch ground cloves

¾ cup of your favorite ground coffee

18 ounces tequila or mezcal

¾ cup whipped cream

12 cinnamon sticks

1 Place the sugar, cinnamon sticks, chocolate, anise seeds, and ground cloves in a 12-cup carafe of a drip coffee pot. Brew 12 cups of your preferred blend of coffee. As the coffee slowly brews, the sugar and chocolate will melt, and the coffee will infuse with the flavor of the spices.

2 Stir after brewing is complete.

3 Add 1½ ounces of tequila or mezcal to a coffee mug. Pour in the hot coffee mixture. Top with a dollop of whipped cream and serve with a cinnamon stick.

WHAT'S IN A NAME?

Translated to "drunken pot of coffee," sugar, chocolate, and spices mask the strength of this fortified eye-opener, so sip with caution.

MI MADRE'S MIGAS TACO   SERVES 5

Yes, I will have tortilla chips in my taco, thank you very much! I adore the toothsome chew of the tortilla chips after they've softened into hot, gooey eggs. For me, the migas (meaning "crumbs") taco is the epitome of comfort food in an edible wrapper and a good reason to save the crumbles in the bottom of the tortilla chip bag. I douse each bite with Valentina hot sauce, so don't even bother setting the bottle down until the last bite is gone. Mi Madre's Migas Taco is simple, satisfying breakfast perfection.

2 tablespoons vegetable oil

½ cup diced tomatoes

½ cup diced onions

¼ cup sliced jalapeños

1 cup tortilla chip strips

10 large eggs, beaten

1 cup shredded Monterey Jack and cheddar cheese blend

5 flour or corn tortillas, warmed

Hot sauce or salsa

1   Preheat the oven to 350°F.

2   Heat the oil in a large skillet over medium heat. Add the tomatoes, onions, jalapeños, and tortilla chip strips. Slowly pour the eggs into the pan. Use a spatula to turn the eggs gently to ensure tortilla strips stay whole. Once eggs are fully cooked, add the cheese to the top. Place the pan in the oven for 3 minutes, or just until the cheese has melted but not browned. Divide the eggs between the warm tortillas to serve.

SANGRITA Y TEQUILA COMPLETO
SERVES 10 (MAKES ABOUT 2½ CUPS)

If you haven't sipped rosy sangrita (not to be confused with sangria), then say hello to a mouthwatering companion for your next shot of tequila. I salivate just thinking about it. Since the early twentieth century, sangrita, which translates to "little blood," has been the classic nonalcoholic sidekick you get when ordering a *completo* in Jalisco, Mexico. The spicy citrus medley's sweet-tart-savory qualities prime the palate and highlight the earthy notes in the tequila. Sip from each shot glass slowly to enjoy the juxtaposition of flavors. While homemade sangrita from freshly squeezed juices is always best, Viuda de Sanchez sangrita mix is a worthy commercial brand if you don't feel like doing the juicing yourself. You sometimes will find tomato-based sangrita served at bars, but that is more of an American thing. Recipes for classic sangrita are as varied as recipes for salsa, but freshly squeezed citrus juices and hot sauce predominate, sometimes gussied up with additions like simple syrup, steeped hibiscus blossoms, or herbs. For hot sauce, I turn to Jalisco-produced Cholula in this sangrita recipe, but use whatever hot sauce lights your fire.

SANGRITA

6 ounces fresh orange or tangerine juice

6 ounces fresh grapefruit juice

6 ounces fresh lime juice

1½ ounces pomegranate juice or grenadine

1 ounce Cholula Hot Sauce

10 ounces blanco tequila

1   Combine the citrus juices, pomegranate juice or grenadine, and hot sauce in a pitcher and stir well to combine. Chill for at least 4 hours.

2   Pour 2 ounces chilled sangrita in a double shot glass. Pour 2 ounces blanco tequila in a second double shot glass. Serve and sip side by side.

SANGRITA COCKTAIL

Combine 8 ounces sangrita and 2 ounces tequila in an ice-filled highball glass. Stir with a bar spoon. Garnish with a lime wedge. Serves 1.

EIGHT ROW FLINT

1039 YALE STREET
HOUSTON HEIGHTS, TX 77008
832.767.4002
AGRICOLEHOSPITALITY.COM

Refuel at Eight Row Flint, an open-air whiskey and taco joint inside an old Citgo filling station that is a modern reinterpretation of the classic icehouse—that totally Texas cross between an open-air saloon and convenience store. Icehouses were a precursor to the drive-thru beer barns of my college days, only decidedly more stop-and-stay-awhile. Born of the pre-refrigeration need for that rare commodity in Texas—ice—customers would stop in to purchase a block of ice for an ice box or cellar, snag a few staples, cool off with a cold drink, and stick around to listen to a fiddle player or the hem and haw of regulars in no hurry to hit the road.

That same stay-awhile vibe permeates Eight Row Flint where patrons linger for inspired sips—a robust selection of whiskeys, beers, and ample spirits of the agave persuasion—and the inspired snacks, tacos, and sides.

Co-owners Chef Ryan Pera and Beverage Director Morgan Weber, the team behind the popular Coltivare and Revival Market, named their third restaurant for a rare, flavorful variety of indigenous corn nearly lost to history. Eight Row Flint corn was used in the earliest distillation of American whiskey and later introduced to Italy, where it became the preferred corn for polenta. Due to its low yield, American farmers turned to other corn crops, and the variety became all but extinct here. Anson Mills's Greg Roberts brought it back to the Americas from Italy to be cultivated again for its sweet corn flavor, protein, and creamy starch. Though the restaurant's focus is an homage to this heirloom, the nixtamalized corn used for the house-made tortillas come from a more readily available organic variety.

The restaurant kitchen is housed in a permanently parked food truck. Grab a seat, a made-to-order cocktail from the frozen drink machines (or order a sophisticated sip from the bar), peruse the menu, and linger. The vegetarian Brussels Sprouts Tacos (page 75) are a surprising customer favorite, this being Texas. Frankly, you can't go wrong with any of the half dozen or so tacos that grace the menu—fried shrimp shellacked with citrus glaze and dotted with black sesame seeds; Thai basil, chicken, and kale with chili mayo and pickled red onion; or luscious Berkshire pork with tart tamarind and charred scallions. This is one filling station where a Slim Jim and a Slurpee could never entice.

RANCHWATER SERVES 1 (photo on Contents Page)

Sometimes referred to as a T&T for tequila and Topo Chico, this is an embellished version of what is arguably the signature cocktail of West Texas. Eight Row Flint's Morgan Weber swaps the tequila with *sotol* (Spanish for "desert spoon"), an agave cousin in the asparagus family that grows in northern Mexico and Texas. Desert Spoon Distillery in Driftwood, Texas, is making sotol from the wild-harvest plants that are native to the area. Weber uses clarified lime juice made with agar in a centrifuge in the bar's Ranchwater. Clarifying allows you to add all the citrus flavor you want to a drink, but with zero cloudiness, and it extends the shelf life of refrigerated juices a bit. Regular lime juice is fine, or try the quick clarification method noted below.

1½ ounces freezer-chilled sotol

¾ ounce lime juice, preferably clarified (see Note below)

½ ounce Lime Oleo-Saccharum (*recipe below*)

2 pinches salt

3 fat strips grapefruit peel

4 ounces Topo Chico sparkling water

Combine all ingredients except Topo Chico in an ice-filled glass. Stir until well chilled. Top with the Topo Chico.

LIME OLEO-SACCHARUM

Remove the peels from 5 small limes with a vegetable peeler or paring knife, avoiding the bitter white pith. Place the peels in a jar and sprinkle with ½ cup sugar. Muddle well with a wooden spoon to grind the sugar into the peels and release the citrus oils. Let sit at room temperature 8 hours, or overnight. Strain, pressing on the peels to extract any remaining oils. Transfer the syrup to a clean bottle. Refrigerate and use within 1 week.

Note: To quick-clarify lime juice, place a fine-mesh strainer lined with a coffee filter over a bowl. Pour 1 cup freshly squeezed lime juice into the strainer, allowing it to percolate through the filter. Walk away, as this can take an hour or more. The filtered juice will be much less cloudy and free of pulp. Makes about 1 cup.

EIGHT ROW FLINT
BRUSSELS SPROUTS TACO SERVES 2

Frying Brussels sprouts turns every child's dinner plate nightmare into something otherworldly and downright addictive. The method unfurls the tender leaves into crispy petals. This is a vegetarian taco that is as substantial as it is sublime. As for any taco, it demands the very best tortillas you can find. Be sure that the Brussels sprouts are thoroughly dry or the oil will splatter violently when they are added to the pan.

1 cup (4 ounces) Brussels sprouts, trimmed

2 ounces watermelon radish, julienned (about ½ cup)

1 tablespoon chopped cilantro

1 tablespoon fresh lime juice

Canola oil for frying

Kosher salt and freshly ground black pepper

4 (5½-inch) flour or corn tortillas

¼ cup sour cream

½ cup crumbled queso fresco

¼ cup coarsely chopped charred onions (see Note)

1 Halve or quarter the Brussels sprouts so that they are uniform and bite-size. Toss the radish with the cilantro and lime juice. Set both aside.

2 Heat about 2 inches of the oil in a deep, heavy skillet or deep fryer until it reaches 350°F. Add the Brussels sprouts and fry, in 2 batches, 3 to 4 minutes until the outer leaves begin to darken and get crispy. Remove them with a slotted spoon to a plate lined with several layers of paper towels to soak up excess oil. Sprinkle with salt and pepper.

3 Spoon the sour cream on each tortilla and sprinkle with the queso fresco. Top with the hot Brussels sprouts and watermelon radish mixture. Sprinkle with the charred onions. Serve immediately.

Note: To make charred onions, cut white onions into thick (½-inch) slices and sear in a blasting hot pan on the stovetop, or on a baking sheet beneath the oven broiler, turning once, until the onions develop a dark char.

77

TEQUILA & TACOS

VELVET TACO

77 W. PACES FERRY ROAD NW, SUITE 35A
ATLANTA, GA 30305
VELVETTACO.COM

What some call appropriation, others see as evolution. Velvet Taco's founders, Randy DeWitt and Jack Gibbons, called their concept "a temple to the liberated taco." Here, chef-inspired tacos, an outlier philosophy, and food made from only the freshest ingredients set Velvet Taco apart in a way that not only bucks tradition but also the mainstream fast-casual taqueria formula. CEO Clay Dover says that they "strive to include two opposing elements—familiarity and surprise" in every taco. The taco shell is quite simply a vehicle for a world of made-from-scratch deliciousness.

VT's diverse menu lets you plot your main course. Take a multi-cultural journey of the taste buds with the customer-favorite Spicy Tikka Chicken taco with cilantro basmati and raita in a flour tortilla; the vegetarian Falafel taco laced with tahini, arugula, pickled peppers, and pea tendrils in a lettuce wrapper; or the Cuban Pig taco loaded with slow-roasted pork, ham, Gruyère, and a pickle in a flour tortilla. For something a bit more familiar, follow the American road and order a soulful Chicken & Waffle taco drizzled with maple syrup, peppercorn gravy, and topped with a bright green apple slaw. Or, try a taco-take on Low Country Shrimp & Grits with creole mayo, charred tomato salsa, and cheesy grits woven together in a corn tortilla. Even the pickiest of eaters will appreciate the Kobe Bacon Burger taco with smoked cheddar and all the fixin's tucked into a flour tortilla. The list of inspired taco hacks goes on and on . . . and so do the Velvet Taco locations. The chain will soon have a dozen restaurants fanning out from its Texas home base to Georgia, North Carolina, and Illinois with a thoughtful plan in place for further expansion.

Of course, you need something to wash all that delicious taco ingenuity down. Choose from a selection of craft beer and soda, or order their boozy Kick-Ass Margarita made with Lunazul Blanco tequila and O3 Orange instead of the traditional triple sec. It gets a dose of sweetness from organic blue agave nectar. It's what I call a velvet sipper!

MEXICAN TEPACHE   SERVES 8 TO 10 (MAKES 2 QUARTS)

In the tequila category, VT serves a mean margarita, but it didn't seem like the ideal match for this brunch-y taco, so they allowed me to come up with an alternative complementary cocktail sidekick. Tepache, a Mexican fermented pineapple drink similar to kombucha, popped to my mind as the backdrop for a bubbly tequila-spiked alternative to the brunchtime mimosa. The fermented juice can be made up to a week in advance and kept refrigerated. Include the jalapeño if you like a little kick.

1 whole pineapple, stemmed and washed

1 cup granulated sugar

1 cup dark brown sugar

1 jalapeño pepper, thinly sliced (optional)

1 cinnamon stick

6 whole cloves

1 Cut the pineapple (skin and core included) into 2-inch cubes. Combine the pineapple and the remaining ingredients with 2 quarts hot water in a large stockpot. Stir to combine. Cover the pot with several layers of cheesecloth. Set aside at room temperature for 24 hours.

2 Remove the cheesecloth and skim away any foam that may have formed on the surface of the liquid. Cover again and let sit, skimming if necessary, until the mixture is sweet and pleasingly fizzy, 24 to 48 hours.

3 Strain the mixture through a cheesecloth-lined strainer into a gallon-size container. Refrigerate and enjoy straight over ice, dilute with water to taste, or make into a cocktail (*recipe follows*).

SPIKED MEXICAN TEPACHE

Add 2 ounces blanco tequila to an ice-filled Collins glass. Add 6 ounces tepache and a squeeze of fresh lime juice. Garnish with a lime wedge and pineapple leaf. Serves 1.

MONTE CRISTO TACO SERVES 2

This recipe is a delicious example of what happens when cooks are given the freedom to play in the kitchen. The folks at Velvet Taco were focused on fleshing out their brunch taco menu when they came up with this taco spin mashup of French Toast and the classic Monte Cristo ham-and-cheese sandwich. From batter to filling to salsa, it's easy to see how the VT chefs thoughtfully packed in flavor at every step.

French Toast Batter
(*recipe follows*)

4 (6-inch) flour tortillas

1 cup grated Gruyère cheese

8 thin slices ham

4 tablespoons strawberry jam

1 tablespoon Strawberry Salsa (*recipe follows*)

4 teaspoons powdered sugar

1 teaspoon micro mint or chopped mint leaves

1 Preheat an electric griddle to 350°F (or heat a cast-iron skillet over medium heat) and spray with cooking pan spray.

2 Dip a flour tortilla in the French Toast Batter. Let soak for 30 seconds. Transfer the tortilla to the hot griddle and cook 1 minute. Flip the tortilla over and immediately cover with ¼ cup of the cheese. Cook for 1 more minute. Remove to a cooling rack while you prepare the remaining tortillas.

3 Place the ham slices flat on the griddle. Cook for 30 seconds per side.

4 Top the melted cheese on each tortilla with 1 tablespoon strawberry jam and 2 pieces of ham. Cover the ham with 1 tablespoon of the Strawberry Salsa and sprinkle with 1 teaspoon powdered sugar and a pinch of micro mint or chopped mint leaves.

FRENCH TOAST BATTER

Whisk together 2 large eggs, ⅔ cup whole milk, 1 teaspoon vanilla extract, and ½ teaspoon ground cinnamon in a mixing bowl. Makes about 1⅓ cups.

STRAWBERRY SALSA

Combine ½ cup diced strawberries with 1 tablespoon seeded and diced jalapeño, and 2 tablespoons diced red onion. Makes about ¾ cup.

ETHIOPIAN INJERA TACO

At Gorsha, in Washington, DC's Union Market, you can order Ethiopian injera bread pockets stuffed with turmeric rice, braised lamb, and pickled shallots or any way you like. Head a thousand miles east to Wisconsin and sample an Ethiopia-meets-Mexico mash-up at the not-for-profit Taste of Ethiopia food truck in Green Bay. There, griddled corn tortillas come spackled with an aromatic paste of slow-cooked garlic, peppers, and fresh ginger cradling mouthwatering braised meats or spiced lentils. Your purchase fights hunger and illiteracy in Ethiopia. Scoot over to the West Coast and seek out Revolutionario in Los Angeles, which serves award-winning North African tacos influenced by French and Arab cuisines. It appears that the humble taco is getting full of itself in all the right ways.

Think of these as rolled tacos in a soft, tangy injera bread wrapper. The longer you ferment the injera batter, the more pronounced the sourness. Let it sit overnight for a tangier final product, or under an hour for milder flavor. The doro wat filling is a classic Ethiopian chicken stew in which a heap of onions gets lazily cooked down with ginger and garlic. The key ingredient is time. The longer you cook the aromatics, the more complex flavor develops. Look for berbere spice at specialty grocers or online, or make your own mix by mixing cayenne, paprika, red chile flakes, garlic, nutmeg, cinnamon, and cloves.

DORO WAT INJERA TACO SERVES 4

6 boneless, skinless chicken thighs

Juice of 1 lemon

2 teaspoons kosher salt

3 small red onions (1½ pounds), peeled and quartered

1 (1-inch) piece peeled ginger

4 garlic cloves, peeled

3 tablespoons ghee

Kosher salt and freshly ground black pepper

3 tablespoons tomato paste

1 tablespoon berbere spice

½ teaspoon ground cinnamon

1 teaspoon ground coriander

1 teaspoon paprika

1 pint chicken stock

Injera Bread (recipe follows)

4 large hard-boiled eggs, peeled and chopped

Toppings: parsley leaves, jalapeño slices, cilantro leaves

1 Toss the chicken thighs in a bowl with the lemon juice and salt to evenly coat. Cover; set aside for 30 minutes.

2 Pulse the onions, ginger, and garlic in a food processor fitted with the metal blade about 12 times or until just finely minced. Heat a Dutch oven over medium-high heat for 1 minute. Add 1½ tablespoons of the ghee. Add the chicken. Cook 3 minutes per side, or until lightly brown. Remove the chicken. Add the remaining 1½ tablespoons ghee, the onion mixture, salt, and pepper. Reduce the heat to low and cook, stirring often, until most of the moisture has evaporated and the onions are caramelized, 15 to 20 minutes.

3 Raise the heat to medium-high. Stir in the tomato paste and spices. Add the chicken stock and bring to a simmer, stirring to scrape up any brown bits from the bottom of the pot. Cover and cook for 25 minutes or until the chicken is cooked through and tender. Stir occasionally. Shred the chicken with two forks and mix into the sauce to combine. Keep warm.

4 Serve the doro wat atop fresh Injera Bread rounds. Garnish with the egg and a sprinkling of parsley leaves, sliced jalapeños, and cilantro leaves.

INJERA BREAD MAKES 8 INJERA ROUNDS

1 cup teff flour

⅛ teaspoon active dry yeast

¼ cup plain yogurt

1 cup water at room temperature

½ cup all-purpose flour

¾ teaspoon baking powder

Pinch kosher salt

1 Mix the teff flour, yeast, yogurt, and water in a mixing bowl until no lumps remain. Cover with a kitchen towel and set the batter aside for 8 hours or up to 36 hours to ferment. (The longer it sits, the more sour the flavor.) The mixture will be bubbly and slightly wet.

2 Once fermented, whisk in the flour, baking powder, and salt. (It will resemble thin pancake batter.)

3 Heat a small nonstick skillet or cast-iron skillet over medium heat for 3 minutes. Pour about ¼ cup batter into the skillet to just cover the surface. Cook for about 30 seconds. Bubbles will form and the sides of the Injera will start to pull away from the pan. Cover the skillet with the lid and let the steam finish cooking the Injera, 1 to 2 minutes more, or until the edges are slightly dry and have just begun to curl. Remove the Injera from the skillet and transfer to a cooling rack while you cook the remaining Injera.

LONA COCINA TEQUILERIA

321 N. FORT LAUDERDALE BEACH BOULEVARD
FORT LAUDERDALE, FL 33304
954.245.3069
LONARESTAURANT.COM

A table by the beach is hard to beat and the view from the patio of Lona is so striking that it's hard to focus on anything else . . . that is, until the food arrives. The young, celebrated Mexican Chef Pablo Salas of destination-restaurant Amaranta in Toluca, Mexico, and the street-casual Público in Mexico City was courted stateside to open this vibrant waterfront restaurant on the ground floor of the Westin Fort Lauderdale Beach Resort. Banish any thought of lackluster hotel food. Like the view, Salas's menu does not disappoint. It is simple, exquisite Mexican fare made by a knowledgeable chef with pristine ingredients.

Beachy starters like citrusy Ceviche Negro tossed with charred guajillo chiles, zesty shrimp cocktail, or tender tuna on a crisp tostada prime the palate for the good things to come. Chef's specials like Braised Beef Cheek in pipian sauce and Salmon Mole with sweet squash and roasted cashews entice, but so do the tacos. How about butter-poached lobster with yellow rice and creamy habanero sauce, or mesquite-smoked chicken al carbon with avocado mousse and tart pickled onions? The most popular taco is Salas's Tacos al Pastor. "On Tuesday's we feature a live Pastor Trompo, which is carved table-side. From the fresh fish in our Ceviche Negro, to the grouper found in our Baja Fish Tacos, we consistently look for opportunities to incorporate local coastal favorites. Menu items are constantly evolving," explains Chef Salas.

After his formal culinary training, Salas spent years studying the ingredients and varied dishes of the state of Mexico, the region of the country he calls home. His mastery of "cocina Mexiquense" has put him in the viewfinder of big-name culinary players and gushing critics who have kept him on best-of lists for years, and the offers for collaborations and business opportunities keep coming.

That's definitely something worth raising a glass to. If you're at Lona, order from the list of almost three hundred tequilas and mezcals offered. "Guests are beginning to appreciate the complexity of agave spirits. Most people are introduced to tequila when they are confronted with a chilled shot of blanco. As you familiarize yourself with the clean and rich flavors of reposado and añejo, you begin to appreciate truly sipping tequila, in addition to the opportunities for cocktail pairings," says General Manager Kira Calder.

If you're miles from Lona, mix up the restaurant's popular Lona Picante (page 88), a smoky mezcal margarita, raise the glass, and say "salud" to Chef Salas.

LONA PICANTE SERVES 1

"Our Lona Picante includes a Jalapeño-Infused Chartreuse…a French liquor that is used in conjunction with Cointreau. Cointreau was the original orange liquor used for the Margarita, when it was created in 1938. This is our version of a spicy margarita and incorporates Volcan Tequila for a smooth, clean mouth-feel, jalapeño for a hint of spice, and Chartreuse for balance and allusion to the Margarita's creation," explains Lona GM, Kira Calder.

1 ounce blanco tequila

1 ounce mezcal

1 ounce fresh lime juice

½-ounce Jalapeño-Infused Green Chartreuse (recipe follows)

½ ounce agave nectar

Pinch of chile salt, such as Tajín

Cucumber wheel

Combine the tequila, mezcal, lime juice, and Chartreuse in a shaker. Shake vigorously. Strain into an ice-filled Collins glass. Add a pinch of chile salt and garnish with a cucumber wheel.

JALAPEÑO-INFUSED GREEN CHARTREUSE

Add 3 to 4 jalapeños that have been stemmed and quartered lengthwise to a 750-ml bottle of green Chartreuse. Let the liqueur steep for 1 to 2 weeks. Strain, discarding solids, and return the infused liqueur to a clean bottle. Keep sealed in a cool, dry place. Makes 750 ml.

BAJA FISH TACOS SERVES 12

At Lona, Chef Salas mixes Mexican crema with lime juice, salt, and pepper to taste to create what is known as *crema fresca*, but you can do the same to brighten sour cream in a pinch.

2 pounds mahi-mahi or grouper

1 quart canola oil

Kosher salt and freshly ground black pepper

BAJA BATTER

2 cups all-purpose flour

12 ounces light Mexican beer

1½ teaspoons Dijon mustard

¼ teaspoon Mexican oregano

½ teaspoon black pepper

½ teaspoon salt

TACO

24 corn tortillas

2 cups shredded cabbage

1 cup Pico de Gallo (*recipe follows*)

Chipotle Aioli (*recipe follows*)

Mexican crema

1 Rinse the fish and pat dry thoroughly. Cut into 12 (2-ounce) portions. Set aside. Heat 1 quart canola oil in a deep fryer to 360°F.

2 Season the fish with salt and pepper. Combine all the ingredients for the Baja Batter and mix well. Dip the fish portions in the batter. Carefully drop the pieces into the hot oil and cook until golden brown, about 2 minutes per side. Transfer to a cooling rack set over a layer of paper towels to drain and cool slightly, about 2 minutes.

3 Place a portion of fish in the center of 2 stacked corn tortillas; top with cabbage, Pico de Gallo, Chipotle Aioli, and the Mexican crema (or crema fresca; see Headnote).

PICO DE GALLO

Stir together 4 diced plum tomatoes, ½ cup diced onion, 3 tablespoons chopped fresh cilantro, 2 tablespoons fresh lime juice, and ½ teaspoon salt. Makes about 2½ cups.

CHIPOTLE AIOLI

Blend 4 chipotle peppers in adobo (⅓ cup) in a blender until smooth. Stir into ¾ cup mayonnaise. Refrigerate until ready to serve. Makes about 1 cup.

TORO TORO

100 CHOPIN PLAZA
MIAMI, FL 33131
305.372.4710
TOROTOROMIAMI.COM

Mexican chef Richard Sandoval is conquering the world one restaurant at a time with nearly fifty establishments in North America, Asia, the Middle East, and Europe. Hospitality runs in his family. His father owned two successful restaurants in Acapulco and his grandmother was an avid cook who put a young Richard to work in the family kitchen as she prepared feasts for the constant gatherings of family and friends.

Before the chef donned a toque, he toted a tennis racket as a pro on the circuit. Traveling to matches exposed him to a world of cuisines beyond his native Mexico. He became so enamored of food and drink that he eventually enrolled in the Culinary Institute of America. Though his first two restaurant ventures focused on French food, he felt compelled to cook, elevate, and share the ingredients of his native Mexico. He opened his flagship restaurant, Maya, in New York in the late '90s. There he developed his signature style of marrying distinctly Latin ingredients with international flavors to create unique, modern menus that garner attention.

There are a handful of Sandoval's Toro Toro restaurants around the world. Each is unique to its locale in both interior design and menu offerings, and not a cookie-cutter replication of a singular concept. Miami's Toro Toro is a Pan-Latin approach to the contemporary steak house led by Executive Chef Jean Delgado, who finds his inspiration from the mosaic of cuisines and cultures the city offers. The restaurant's name is an ecumenical nod to surf and turf. Toro is both the Japanese word for "tuna" and the Spanish word for "bull," and you will find the menu melds Asian, Latin, seafood, and steak at every turn.

"At Toro Toro, we look at what is in season and how we can incorporate these ingredients into our dishes. A lot of our inspiration comes from family recipes . . . we always try to bring out flavors that remind us of home, while still giving them an elevated touch. As long as it tastes delicious, nothing is off-limits," explains Chef Delgado.

Order from an array of hot or cold tapas-style small plates or pick a large meaty entrée and a few sides. If your table goes for the rodizio-style Churrasco experience, everyone gets to sample as much as they want from the grill, but also sides and small plates too. Tuesdays are perhaps the most popular night, and it's all about the tacos. The lineup includes taco standards with Toro Toro twists like the Al Pastor tacos with Tangy Chili Sauce, Flank Steak tacos with Queso Fresco and Ají Amarillo, and the enduring crowd-favorite: Crispy Shrimp Tacos with Avocado and a homemade Jalapeño Ranch drizzle.

NEGRITA SERVES 1

Sandoval's passion for agave spirits has led him to cultivate one of the largest collections in North America. This dramatic drink shows how well tequila plays with fruit.

5 blackberries

1 ounce pineapple juice

1 ounce freshly squeezed lime juice

¾ ounce agave syrup

2 ounces Avion tequila

Splash of blue curaçao

Orchid blossom

Muddle the blackberries in an ice-filled shaker tin. Add the pineapple juice, lime juice, agave syrup, tequila, and blue curaçao. Cover and shake vigorously. Strain into a martini glass and garnish with an orchid blossom.

WHAT'S IN A NAME?

Negrita means "bold" and seemed a fitting name for a tequila cocktail that is bold, distinctive, and an unforgettable hue thanks to the stain of muddled blackberries and blue curaçao. A bartender warns, "If you have just the right amount of Negritas, you'll be feeling pretty bold yourself!"

LOBSTER TACOS SERVES 4

Chef Delgado serves these as appetizer-size mini tacos at the Toro Toro bar.
Use leftover Rocoto Aioli as a delicious sauce for grilled lamb or roasted salmon.

About 10 ounces frozen raw lobster claw and knuckle meat, thawed (or 4 lobster tails)

½ cup butter, cubed

ROCOTO AIOLI

2 tablespoons ají rocoto red hot pepper paste, such as Goya brand

1 (16-ounce) jar roasted red bell peppers, drained and julienned

1 tablespoon minced fresh ginger

1 teaspoon sliced garlic

½ cup plus 1 tablespoon olive oil

2 (2 × ½-inch) strips lemon peel, boiled in water until softened

⅓ cup white balsamic vinegar

2 teaspoons honey

2 tablespoons water

1 tablespoon Dijon mustard

1 teaspoon kosher salt

Juice of 1 lemon

Kosher salt

8 hard corn taco shells

Crème Fraîche Coleslaw (recipe follows)

8 avocado slices

Pinch micro cilantro leaves or chopped fresh cilantro

4 lemon wedges

1   Place a 3½-quart saucepan over medium heat. Add water to come 2 inches up the sides of the pan. Add the butter, bring to a boil, and reduce the heat to a simmer. Add the lobster meat to the pan with liquid to cover. Poach for 4 to 6 minutes or until just firm.

2   Remove the cooked lobster meat with a slotted spoon and place in an ice bath to cool quickly.

3   Meanwhile, make the aioli: In a saucepan, sauté the pepper paste and roasted peppers, ginger, and garlic in 1 tablespoon of the olive oil on low heat until very tender. Cool slightly. Transfer the pepper mixture, lemon peel, vinegar, honey, water, mustard, and salt in a blender and blend for 1 to 2 minutes on high until finely pureed. With the blender running, slowly add the ½ cup olive oil through the hole in the lid until the aioli is emulsified and creamy.

4   Mix the chilled lobster with 1½ cups plus 3 tablespoons of the aioli, the lemon juice, and season with salt.

5   Fill the taco shells with the lobster mixture, Crème Fraîche Coleslaw, and avocado slices. Top with cilantro and serve with lemon wedges.

CRÈME FRAÎCHE COLESLAW

Whisk together ½ cup crème fraîche, 2 tablespoons buttermilk, ½ teaspoon champagne vinegar, and 1 teaspoon finely grated lemon zest to combine. Toss the dressing with a mix of 2 cups shredded green cabbage and 1 cup shredded red cabbage. Season with ½ teaspoon kosher salt. Makes about 2½ cups.

3

MIDWEST

THE RESTAURANTS

MISSION TACO JOINT

6235 DELMAR BOULEVARD
ST. LOUIS, MO 63130
314.932.5430
MISSIONTACOJOINT.COM

Brothers Adam and Jason Tilford grew up in a coast guard family living all over the country, but mostly on the West Coast. They now call the Midwest home, but they've been sharing tastes of the Golden State with Missouri and Kansas diners for over a decade. First with Tortillaria and Milagro restaurants and now with eight Mission Taco Joints where they sling "Mexican fare with California flair."

The brothers chose to focus on the style of taco truck fare they loved back in California. "We're pure West Coast, and saw an opening for bringing this colorful vibe to our little spot in the Midwest," Adam explains. The name is an homage to San Francisco's Mission District, where old-school taquerias mix with chef-driven eateries and craft cocktail lounges.

The menu reflects that blend of low-key and luxe. As Mission Taco Joint's chef, Jason sees the taco as a great vessel for exploring techniques. "I like to combine savory with sweet, spicy, tangy . . . texture-wise you always have to have some crunch," he says. "We do an autumnal taco in the fall, usually based on a sweet potato hash. We put out a seafood taco during Lent, sometimes bringing back a classic mahi-mahi guest favorite, or coming up with something new, like this year's salmon taco that was grilled in a banana leaf. We often do collaborations with local restaurants, and let the guest chef pick a charity to which we will donate a portion of that taco's sales. One of our favorites was a phở taco we did with Qui from Mai Lee, and coming up we are working on a Cuban sandwich taco with Wil from Rock Star Taco Shack." Beyond the specials and collaborations, there are fixtures like the Mango-Hop-Anero-Shrimp taco. The shrimp gets dipped in a Mexican beer batter and fried to perfection before getting accessorized with mango salsa and habanero aioli. "During our busy season we can sell up to 37,000 shrimp tacos in a month!" Jason exclaims.

The MTJ bar offers an array of tequila and mezcal cocktails to complement the menu offerings. Beverage Director Kyle Harlan explains that part of his job is asking patrons a lot of questions to determine what drink direction to take them in. "Mezcal has so many different flavor profiles and a lot more freedom in how it can be produced . . . you can find flavors that more people like and will appreciate than with tequilas. I've found that a tequila drinker is a tequila drinker, but with mezcal there is a lot more nuance." You'll find plenty of that flavorful nuance in his Mole Punch cocktail (page 100) too.

MOLE PUNCH SERVES 1

Dark, rich, and swimming with smoke and umami, MTJ Beverage Director Kyle Harlan's mole spin on the Bloody Mary swaps a tequila and mezcal medley for the usual vodka. It's a cocktail that is ripe with surprises: the sweetness of pineapple and chocolate syrup, the spice of jalapeño, smokiness of chipotle, and dashes of complexity from ancho liqueur, allspice dram, bitters, and Maggi seasoning. This is a fun one for a blind tasting—guaranteed no taster will guess all that's in this mix.

Tajín spice (see Note)

3 slices fresh jalapeño

1 ounce Una Vida reposado tequila

½ ounce El Buho mezcal

1 ounce Michelada Mix (*recipe follows*)

1 ounce Abuelita chocolate syrup

1 ounce fresh pineapple juice

½ ounce Ancho Reyes liqueur

½ ounce allspice dram

4 dashes Angostura bitters

2 dashes Maggi Jugo seasoning

1 Rub the rim of a rocks glass with a dampened fingertip and invert the glass on a small plate covered with the Tajín spice. Give a twist to lightly coat the rim.

2 Muddle 1 jalapeño in the bottom of a shaker tin. Add the rest of the ingredients with ice and shake vigorously. Double strain over a cocoa strainer into a rocks glass without ice. Serve up.

MICHELADA MIX

Finely mince 1 chipotle chile in adobo sauce until it is a paste (about 2 teaspoons). Add the chipotle paste to 1 liter of STOUT Bloody Mary Blend mixed with 2 cups freshly squeezed lime juice and 10 ounces agave syrup. Makes about 1 gallon.

Note: Tajín spice is a commercially available proprietary blend of dried ground chile powders, salt, and dehydrated lime juice. It is called "salsa en polvo" in Spanish.

BBQ DUCK TACO SERVES 4 TO 6

This duck taco was inspired by the duck confit tostadita that was served at Milagro, the upscale Mexican restaurant concept the Tilfords used to own. This might as well be called "pato carnitas" because like pork carnitas, here duck, or *pato* in Spanish, is slow-cooked in its own fat until it becomes satiny, succulent, and shreddable. You will appreciate Jason's free-spirited approach to traditional taco components. Instead of the requisite salsa, dried chiles are woven into a complex tart-sweet barbecue sauce, and the usual white onion gets sliced and pickled purple in a tart hibiscus vinegar for a garnish that will have you tickled pink. If that wasn't enough, they gild the taco lily with rich croutons of pork fat. The result is a taco so delicious, it will become your mission to return for more.

½ chipotle chile in adobo, minced to puree

1 tablespoon minced garlic

1½ teaspoons sea salt

½ cup vegetable oil

4 skin-on, bone-in duck leg quarters

2 cups chicken stock

½ cup duck fat (optional)

ANCHO AGAVE BBQ SAUCE
2 ancho chiles

¼ cup chopped white onion

1 cup vegetable stock

2 tablespoons tomato paste

¼ cup dark agave nectar

Corn tortillas, warmed

Avocado, peeled, seeded, and mashed

Hibiscus Pickled Onions (*recipe follows*)

Crisp Pork Belly Carnitas (*recipe follows*)

1 Combine the chipotle, garlic, salt, and oil. Spread the mixture over the duck portions. Refrigerate for 24 hours. Bring the duck to room temperature before cooking.

2 Preheat the oven to 225°F. Arrange the duck pieces in a roasting pan with the stock and fat, if using. Cook for 2½ hours or until the duck is fall-off-the-bone tender.

3 Meanwhile, make the BBQ sauce. Toast the chiles in a searing hot skillet for 25 seconds per side until fragrant. Transfer the toasted chiles to a small bowl, cover with hot water for 15 minutes; drain and rinse twice. Carefully remove the stems and seeds from the rehydrated chiles. Combine the chiles and the remaining ingredients in a small saucepan. Bring to a boil and then reduce the heat to a simmer; cook for 5 minutes. Transfer the sauce to a blender and puree until smooth.

4 Remove the duck from the pan, reserving the cooking liquid. Let the duck rest until cool enough to handle. Remove the skin and bones; discard. Carefully shred the meat and place in a small bowl. Add a little of the cooking liquid to moisten it.

5 Spread a bit of mashed avocado on each tortilla, top with the shredded duck, a spoonful of ancho sauce, Hibiscus Pickled Onions, and a few pieces of the Pork Belly Carnitas.

HIBISCUS PICKLED ONIONS

Boil 1 cup apple cider vinegar, 1½ cups water, 1 tablespoon
sea salt, ¼ cup sugar, and ½ cup dried hibiscus flowers
in a small saucepan over high heat for 5 minutes. Slice
1 medium white onion into rings and place them in a bowl.
Strain the hot liquid over the onion; set aside for at least
2 hours. Drain before use. Makes about ¾ cup.

CRISP PORK BELLY CARNITAS

Cook ¼ pound diced smoked pork belly (slab bacon)
in a small skillet with 2 tablespoons vegetable oil over
medium heat for 10 minutes, or until most of the fat has
rendered and the cubes are crisp. Remove the pork belly
and drain on a plate lined with paper towels. Makes about
½ cup.

CONDADO TACOS

1227 N. HIGH STREET
COLUMBUS, OHIO 43201
614.928.3909
CONDADOTACOS.COM

Don't underestimate that busboy clearing the table behind you. He may be soaking in all the important details to one day become CEO of your favorite restaurant chain. That was the case for Condado Tacos' CEO, Joe Kahn. He got his start bussing tables at a Sizzler in Chicago and worked his way up the restaurant ladder from busboy to dishwasher to server—even waiter on roller skates—to bartender. A bartending job near Wrigley Field coaxed him back to the Midwest from Boulder, Colorado, where he'd been living. A role consulting on new restaurant concepts soon followed.

Over the years, Joe formulated and fine-tuned the vision he had for his own "joint," an affordable, community-focused taco "dispensary" where customers could build tacos by adding a "dab" of this or a dollop of that from a list of fillings and garnishes. Or, they could choose from a melting "pot" menu brimming with delicious "edibles." In 2014, his "pipe" dream came true with his first Condado Tacos on High Street (of course!) in Columbus, Ohio. Today, there are outlets in Ohio, Pennsylvania, Indiana, and Michigan, each painted by local artists with graffiti motifs that feel as much an homage to the Grateful Dead as the *Day of the Dead.*

Perhaps it was his time in Boulder or the influence of his aging-hippie father, but what Joe created is like a countercultural response to the mainstream fast-casual taqueria. The psychedelic interior, inviting bar, and anything-goes taco menu reflect the sort of places where Joe likes to hang out, and it appears locals do, too. Memorable wink-and-nod references to stoner culture can be found in rotating specials like a biscuit-and-gravy breakfast taco called The Wake and Bake, and menu standards like the 'shroom-packed Dutch Dragon or pulled pork, smoked cheddar, and BBQ sauce—laced Bubba Kush (page 106).

The bar offers nearly one hundred bottles of tequila and mezcal and an extensive cocktail menu with options like an Añejo Manhattan (page 105). Choose from a lengthy list of specialty margaritas, or create your own with a flavored add-in. Weeknight happy hours give customers a chance to sip half-priced margaritas and sample the goods with one-buck tacos, assuring no one leaves with an empty stomach or wallet. Now that's pretty dope!

AÑEJO MANHATTAN SERVES 1

The Manhattan is a classic cocktail that originated in the Big Apple, but the who-what-where-story specifics are unverifiable and varied. Traditionally made with whiskey, sweet vermouth, and Angostura bitters, this rendition is made with barrel-aged tequila. Some consider it sacrilege to drink a good aged tequila any way but neat, but the Manhattan showcases the woodsy barrel flavor of long-rested añejos. Where the whiskey Manhattan is a substantial classic that's a sublime closer to an evening on the town, the aged tequila Manhattan delivers oaky notes from the barrel along with the distinctive nuances of agave that party well with sweet vermouth and the nutty bitters used here. The result is a tipple that's a dangerously easy sip to both start and finish the night.

1½ ounces Hornitos Black Barrel añejo tequila

¾ ounce sweet vermouth

½ ounce (splash) Grand Marnier

2 dashes black walnut bitters

Orange peel strip

Maraschino cherry, preferably Luxardo

Combine the tequila, vermouth, Grand Marnier, and bitters in an ice-filled mixing glass. Stir with a bar spoon for 10 seconds to chill. Strain into a 10-ounce rocks glass and serve with a strip of orange peel and a cherry.

BUBBA KUSH TACOS MAKES 6 TACOS (4 TO 6 SERVINGS)

This double-walled taco is an attention-getter and taste bud–teaser. Condado glues a soft flour and hard corn shell together with their house-made refried beans cooked with bacon and jalapeño, but you can gussy up canned refried beans to use in a similar way. The pulled pork in this taco gets a drizzle of Condado's proprietary jackfruit barbecue sauce—a recipe that they prefer to keep close to the poncho, so to speak. Substitute your favorite spicy barbecue sauce instead.

6 (8-inch) flour tortillas

6 hard corn taco shells

1½ cups refried beans

⅓ cup fresh guacamole

⅓ cup sour cream

1½ cups pulled pork

3 tablespoons spicy barbecue sauce

Jicama Slaw (recipe follows)

6 tablespoons chopped white onion

6 tablespoons chopped fresh cilantro

Pineapple Salsa (recipe follows)

¾ cup shredded Middlefield smoked cheddar cheese

1 Make Condado's taco shell by spreading ¼ cup refried beans in the center of each tortilla. Alongside the refried beans, still near the center of the shell, spread 1 tablespoon guacamole and 1 tablespoon sour cream to create a mound of edible "spackle" for the double-walled taco shell. Set the base of the corn shell in the center of the flour shell on the mound of ingredients and bring up the sides of the flour tortilla so that it adheres to the bean-guac-cream mixture and the corn shell.

2 Fill the corn shell with the pulled pork and barbecue sauce. Top with some Jicama Slaw, 1 tablespoon each of onion and cilantro, some Pineapple Salsa, and sprinkle with the smoked cheddar cheese.

JICAMA SLAW

Combine ⅔ cup shredded cabbage, ⅔ cup shredded carrot, and ⅔ cup shredded peeled jicama. Add ⅓ cup thinly sliced red onion and 2 tablespoons chopped fresh cilantro to taste. Fold in 2 tablespoons salt-roasted pepitas (hulled pumpkin seeds). Shake 3 tablespoons unseasoned rice vinegar, 3 tablespoons olive oil, 1 tablespoon minced jalapeño, and salt and pepper to taste in a small jar to emulsify; pour over the slaw to dress. Makes about 2 cups (enough for 6 tacos).

PINEAPPLE SALSA

Combine ½ cup each diced fresh pineapple, diced green bell pepper, diced red bell pepper, diced red onion, and seeded and diced Roma tomatoes. Add 2 tablespoons chopped fresh cilantro, and salt and pepper to suit your taste. Makes 2¼ cups.

INDIAN PARATHA TACOS

Like a flour tortilla with the flaky, buttery goodness of a croissant, pan-fried East Indian paratha bread makes a perfect pliable cradle for most any fillings you choose. The trick is building layers of dough and butter as for a puff pastry, by brushing a layer of melted ghee (clarified butter) on the surface of the dough before it is folded on itself. The technique lends rich flavor and a crispy crunch to an Indian specialty that translates beautifully to tacos. A vegetarian filling of chickpeas and cauliflower seasoned with warm curry spices finds a cooling counterpoint in cool cucumber raita, in a taco spin that pays homage to the roots of its wrapper. Paratha tacos have all of the components we crave: crunch, salt, fat, spice, and a savory filling. For optimal crunch and flavor, these are best filled and served as soon as the paratha is done cooking. Though not as rich or flaky, you can substitute grilled naan or chapati flatbread here.

CURRIED-CAULIFLOWER PARATHA TACOS

MAKES 8 TACOS

PARATHA DOUGH

1 cup whole wheat flour

2 cups all-purpose flour

2 teaspoons kosher salt

2 tablespoons vegetable oil

1 cup water

6 to 8 tablespoons melted ghee for brushing dough

1 can chickpeas, rinsed and drained

1 head cauliflower, cut into small florets

6 tablespoons extra virgin olive oil or ghee

1 teaspoon kosher salt

1 tablespoon ground cumin

1 teaspoon curry powder

1 tablespoon ground turmeric

1 teaspoon red pepper flakes

Raita (*recipe follows*)

Toppings: cilantro leaves, cucumber matchsticks, and fresh jalapeño slices (optional)

1 Combine the flours, salt, and oil in a mixing bowl. Rub the mixture with your hands until it has a soft, sandy texture, about 2 minutes. Slowly add water in small amounts until no dry bits of flour remain. Knead the dough for 2 to 3 minutes until it is smooth and elastic. Divide it into 8 equal pieces and roll each into a ball. Cover with a damp kitchen towel for 30 minutes.

2 On a lightly floured surface, roll each ball of dough into a 4 x 9-inch rectangle. Brush each rectangle of dough with melted ghee all the way to the edges. Tightly roll each rectangle of dough into a rope, rolling from one long edge to the other. Coil each rope into a tight spiral about 3 inches in diameter. Cover the dough with a damp kitchen towel. Let rest 30 minutes.

3 Meanwhile, preheat the oven to 425°F. Thoroughly dry the chickpeas between layers of paper towels. Place the cauliflower and chickpeas in a large bowl. Add the olive oil, salt, cumin, curry powder, turmeric, and red pepper and stir to mix well. (Avoid using your hands, as turmeric stains). Transfer the seasoned cauliflower to a foil-lined baking sheet. Bake for 25 to 30 minutes until cooked through and slightly charred.

4 Heat a cast-iron skillet over medium-high heat for 1 minute. Place a dough spiral on a lightly floured surface. Dust the top with flour and roll it out into a 6-inch circle, flipping the dough on the surface as you roll to ensure that it doesn't stick.

5 Cook the dough in the hot skillet for 1 minute. Brush the top with a bit of melted ghee and flip it over; cook for 30 seconds. (The ghee will smoke, so turn on your exhaust fan). Brush the top with ghee and flip again. Cook until both sides are cooked through with some charred spots. Keep warm and immediately move to the next step.

6   Spread 1 tablespoon of the Raita on the bottom of each Paratha round. Add the cauliflower-chickpea filling. Garnish with cilantro leaves, cucumber matchsticks, and jalapeño slices, if desired.

RAITA

Combine ½ cup full-fat Greek yogurt, ½ English cucumber, finely chopped, the juice of 1 lime (2 tablespoons), ¼ cup chopped cilantro, and kosher salt to taste in a bowl. Makes about 1 cup.

THE HOPPY GNOME

203 E. BERRY STREET
FORT WAYNE, IN 46802
260.422.0070
HOPPYGNOME.COM

Step into The Hoppy Gnome and you've entered what *Architectural Digest* called "the most beautiful bar in Indiana." Equally impressive is the bountiful beer selection, menu of creative cocktails, and the deliciously inauthentic tacos.

Indiana natives, college buddies, and co-owners Peter Shuey and James Khan followed divergent paths in the restaurant business before they eventually crossed again. Together they came up with a concept focused on craft beer and fresh pub fare. Tacos came into the picture by happenstance after they enjoyed a "family meal" of them before service at one of their sister restaurants. "We were in the kitchen inhaling these delicious handheld masterpieces and it just kind of clicked. We all looked at each other and thought 'What about tacos and beer?' We had seen plenty of beer places that combined with burgers, pizza, wings, etcetera, but never one with tacos. Our chef and partner had a menu drawn up the next day, and the rest was history," Peter explains.

The entirely-from-scratch kitchen prepares every component of every dish. Comforting soups and stick-to-your-ribs sides like Chicken Pozole in rich red chile broth and a Paprika Poblano Potato Mash, and entrees with clever names like "The Porkshank Redemption" entice, but it's the tacos that deliver an epiphany in every bite. Order two or three wrapped in your choice of Bibb lettuce, flour, or corn tortillas. "We wanted a way to introduce new, exciting, international flavors in a fun and affordable fashion. The fact that tacos go well with beer also helped," Shuey shares. "We offer guests the option of mixing and matching . . . you can have Asian, Jamaican, and Southern USA all on one plate!"

The bar boasts beer from across the Midwest as well as Germany and Belgium with some forty varieties on tap. If you want to try your hand at brewmaster, you can make an appointment at Gnometown Brewery next door to concoct your own microbrew. They'll store it, bottle it, and add a personalized label, too. Sure, beer features most prominently in this hoppy place, but the handcrafted cocktail menu is a fecund assortment of sublime sips with even more imaginative names, like Unforeseen Conseaquenches (elderflower liqueur, reposado tequila, lemon and lime juices topped with Seaquench Ale), a perfectly on point 35mm Margarita made with Lunazul reposado and a house-made margarita mix that is served with a halo of chile-lime salt gracing the rim. Or sample the Lady Stark (page 113), a floral-and-citrus infused sour made from blanco tequila blended with sweet shiraz right at home.

THE LADY STARK SERVES 1

Wine continues to make a splash in the cocktails in this book, and this homage-in-a-glass to *Game of Thrones* goes complex and deep like the series. Created by former manager Johnny Perez and finessed by resident mixologist Andy Gelwicks, a wine and sweet almond syrup reduction provides the backbone to this smoky mezcal sour with herbal, spice, and floral notes. It's as aromatic (though much headier) than a fine perfume.

2 ounces Stark Mix (*recipe follows*)

½ ounce fresh lemon juice

1 ounce egg white

3 dashes lavender bitters

1¼ ounce Del Maguey Vida mezcal

Jalapeño slice

Mint sprig

Combine the Stark Mix, lemon juice, and egg white in a shaker tin. Dry shake without ice. Add the bitters and mezcal and top with ice. Shake to mix and chill. Strain over fresh ice in a rocks glass. Serve with a jalapeño slice and mint sprig.

STARK MIX

Combine 2 cups sweet shiraz and 2 cups orgeat in a saucepan. Whisk over low to medium heat for 15 to 20 minutes until a bit concentrated and slightly thick.

LEMONGRASS PORK MEATBALL TACOS
MAKES 19 TACOS (SERVES 8 TO 10)

Savory and flavor-packed, these Thai-inspired tacos are poised to displace the Bob Marley and Korean short rib tacos as the new customer favorite at The Hoppy Gnome. Make a double batch of meatballs. Once they've cooled completely after cooking, transfer the baking sheet to the freezer for 1 hour. Transfer the individually frozen meatballs to a zippered freezer bag to pull out and reheat whenever you get a hankering for this taco.

PORK MEATBALLS

1 tablespoon minced lemongrass

2 tablespoons, plus 1 teaspoon minced fresh ginger

2 medium shallots, minced (about 5 tablespoons)

2 pounds chilled ground pork

1 cup panko bread crumbs

2½ tablespoons fish sauce

1 tablespoon kosher salt

2 teaspoons cracked black pepper

38 white or yellow corn tortillas

Red Curry Mayonnaise (*recipe follows*)

Mango Slaw (*recipe follows*)

1 Chill a mixing bowl.

2 Combine the lemongrass, ginger, and shallots and transfer to the bowl of a food processor fitted with the metal blade. Pulse 6 to 8 times until very finely minced. Transfer the mixture to the chilled mixing bowl.

3 Add the chilled pork, panko, fish sauce, salt, and pepper. Gently combine by hand until all the ingredients are incorporated. (The mixture should remain very cold. Do not overmix.) Cover and place in the refrigerator for at least 6 hours.

4 Preheat the oven to 375°F.

5 Portion the mixture into 19 golf ball–size meatballs (about 2 tablespoons). Arrange them on a parchment-lined baking sheet and bake in the oven for 20 minutes.

6 Meanwhile, place the tortillas in a hot cast-iron skillet or grill pan to brown lightly on both sides. Transfer the tortillas to a plate, cover with plastic wrap, and set aside until ready to serve.

7 Remove the meatballs from the oven and check for doneness. (Cut one open to expose the center. It should be cooked through, but not dry.) Tent lightly with aluminum foil to keep the meatballs warm while you assemble the tacos.

8 Place 2 warm tortillas on top of each other. Slice a meatball into quarters. Arrange the 4 pieces of meatball in the double-stacked tortilla. Spoon 1 tablespoon Red Curry Mayonnaise over the meat. Top with about 3 tablespoons of the Mango Slaw. Serve warm.

RED CURRY MAYONNAISE

Blend ¾ teaspoon finely minced garlic, 1 cup mayonnaise, 2 tablespoons fresh lime juice, and 1 tablespoon Thai red curry paste to combine. Refrigerate in a covered container for at least 2 hours before using. Store up to 1 week in the refrigerator. Makes about 1 cup.

MANGO SLAW

Peel and seed 1 large mango and ½ large red bell pepper, and cut into matchsticks. Halve 1 English cucumber crosswise and cut into matchsticks. Halve ½ medium red onion vertically and cut into thin half-moon slices. Combine with ¼ cup chopped cilantro, 2 tablespoons fresh lime juice, 1½ teaspoons honey, and ½ teaspoon kosher salt in a bowl, cover, and refrigerate for 1 hour to allow the flavors to come together. Store up to 2 days in the refrigerator. Makes about 3½ cups.

QUIOTE

Closed late 2019. Enjoy the recipes from these amazing talents and follow them for the latest announcements on Instagram: @thesalsatruck @ross_henke @jameseschroeder

The Salsa Truck, an insanely popular mobile taco stand with a brick-and-mortar extension called the Garage in Chicago's West Loop, gave chef and owner Dan Salls a platform for tinkering with the techniques and traditions of the Mexican food he loved. When the landlord forced him to pull the door down on the Garage, Salls looked at it as an opportunity to put "years of research and a desire to continue to push" into an entirely new venture. In Quiote, and basement mezcaleria Todos Santos, he and his partners, Executive Chef Ross Henke and Beverage Director Jay Schroeder, found outlets to forge ahead and share with diners and drinkers something entirely new on the Chicago food and beverage scene.

That Quiote is named for the towering flowering stalk that agave send up when ready to reproduce, seems fitting for a restaurant that exemplifies rebirth in location, menu, and approach. The food served isn't a complete departure from traditional Mexican fare, rather they describe it as "unbridled interpretations of Mexican classics with fine-dining touches." It is food born of creative passion and love of place. Diners will recognize the ingredients of Chicago and the Midwest as much as the flavors and dishes of Mexico.

"Our mission is more than just an expanded take on a cuisine that we love," says Salls. "We are here to help cultivate the Chicago restaurant industry and to be advocates for our employees and community." Not only do they source ingredients from nearby farms and artisanal purveyors, they also offer homegrown treasures from the restaurant's rooftop garden and honey from the beehives.

The restaurant offers just one taco plate on the dinner menu, an otherworldly Lamb Carnitas Taco (page 118) layered with eggplant salsa verde, cotija, and tahini crema. If customers crave more taco options, they can find them at the Salsa Truck, which is now parked downstairs on Todos Santos's patio. There, you can get late-night fortification in carne asada, pork carnitas, chicken thigh in salsa verde, or rajas with potato tacos washed down with some magical mezcal, bacanora, sotol, or raicilla elixir like Schroeder's Geodesic Domes (page 117). One thing you won't find behind the bar: tequila. Instead, Todos Santos showcases the nuances of agave spirits made with more sustainable agave varieties that are produced using traditional methods.

GEODESIC DOMES SERVES 1

There is no denying that Jay Schroeder is an agave spirits enthusiast. "Mezcal is empirically the coolest spirit that has ever existed, and I will continue saying that until someone challenges me to a duel about it," he exclaims. Todos Santos is the place to get educated, and Jay is the expert you want to school you. A Rick Bayless veteran, Schroeder penned *Understanding Mezcal*, a book that dives deep and wide into the cultivation and distillation of agave. It's a worthy addition to every mezcal-lover's bookshelf.

¾ ounce fresh lemon juice

2¾ ounce Domes Mix (*recipe follows*)

1 ounce Pierre Ferrand 1840

1 ounce Banhez Mezcal

WHAT'S IN A NAME?

Jay Schroeder explains, "The name is inspired by Buckminster Fuller, architect, inventor, and all-around genius. As much as I wish there were a deep connection between the drink's ingredients and the cocktail's name, it's a closely guarded secret that most cocktail folk have a running list of things that would make good names. This one dropped off my list real quick, as it was a good fit for this particular tropical concoction."

Combine all the ingredients in an ice-filled shaker tin. Strain into a wood tumbler over fresh ice to serve.

DOMES MIX

Combine 9 ounces pineapple puree, 3 ounces cardamom clove syrup, 3 ounces Cinzano bianco vermouth, and 1½ ounces Fernet Branca. Store in a bottle in the refrigerator for up to 1 week. Makes 16½ ounces (enough for 6 drinks).

LAMB CARNITAS TACO MAKES 8 TACOS (SERVES 4)

This taco is a revelation and the only taco offered on the dinner menu at Quiote. Chef Henke confits lamb sourced from nearby Catalpa Grove Farm. The flour tortilla wrapper, nuggets of eggplant, and a crema blended with sesame tahini conjure the OG al pastor taco that Lebanese immigrants to Veracruz introduced to Mexico. Use any leftover salsa as a cheese or charcuterie accoutrement. Chef Henke suggests folding in some grainy mustard "for a unique mostarda."

2 pounds boneless lamb shoulder, cubed

Kosher salt

2 quarts lard (pork fat)

2 tablespoons canola oil

8 corn tortillas

Salsa Verde Eggplant (recipe follows)

Tahini Crema (recipe follows)

½ cup crumbled cotija or queso fresco

¼ cup chopped cilantro

Lime wedges

1 Season the cubed lamb with salt. Cover and refrigerate at least 8 hours or overnight.

2 Preheat the oven to 325°F.

3 Melt the lard in a Dutch oven over medium-high heat. Add the lamb cubes. Cover and transfer the pot to the oven. Cook 2½ hours or until the meat is tender but not falling apart.

4 Remove the pot from the oven and separate the lamb from the pork fat with a slotted spoon, reserving the pork fat for later use.

5 Heat the oil in a nonstick pan over medium-high heat until you see wisps of smoke. Working in batches, carefully add the cooked lamb cubes and fry until crispy. Drain on a layer of paper towels.

6 Warm the tortillas on a griddle plate or over a burner. Top each tortilla with a spoonful or two of the eggplant salsa and arrange cubes of the crispy lamb down the center. Drizzle the lamb with Tahini Crema. Finish with a sprinkling of cheese and cilantro. Serve with lime wedges.

TAHINI CREMA

Whisk together 1 cup sour cream, ¼ cup tahini paste, and 1 teaspoon salt in a bowl. Makes 1¼ cups.

SALSA VERDE EGGPLANT

MAKES ABOUT 4½ CUPS

- 10 tomatillos, skinned and quartered
- 1 serrano chile, seeds and ribs removed
- 3 garlic cloves
- 1 white onion, quartered
- ¼ cup apple cider vinegar
- 2 tablespoons honey
- 2 tablespoons soy sauce
- 1 tablespoon kosher salt
- ¼ cup, plus 2 tablespoons canola oil
- 4 Japanese eggplants

1 Preheat the oven to 500°F.

2 Blend the tomatillos, chile, garlic, onion, vinegar, honey, soy, salt, and ¼ cup of the canola oil in a blender until smooth.

3 Cut the eggplant into 1-inch pieces. Toss the pieces with the remaining 2 tablespoons canola oil and arrange on a baking sheet. Place the baking sheet in the oven and roast until the eggplant is dark brown, 15 to 20 minutes.

4 As soon as you take the eggplant out of the oven, combine it with the marinade so that it absorbs the flavor. Set aside.

THE EL DIABLO SERVES 1

Tequila often gets a bad rap, whether it's a country singer crooning that "you and tequila make me crazy" or the fact that many imbibers believe various spirits have markedly different effects on their demeanor. Many label tequila as the worst of the boozy beverage bunch. Perhaps that wicked reputation is how the American-born "Mexican El Diablo" cocktail got its name. It is thought to have first appeared in print in the classic *Trader Vic's Book of Food & Drink* of 1946. The original recipe called for blanco tequila, but over the years bartenders have mixed up El Diablos using aged tequilas for the complexity they provide. A good reposado or añejo can stand up to the bold bite of ginger beer. Or go bolder with a mezcal-laced Smoky Devil.

2 ounces blanco or reposado tequila

½ ounce fresh lime juice

½ ounce crème de cassis

3 ounces ginger beer

Lime wheel

Skewer of fresh currants or blackberries

Combine the tequila, lime juice, and crème de cassis in an ice-filled shaker tin. Strain over fresh ice in a highball glass. Top with ginger beer and stir with a bar spoon. Serve with a lime wheel and skewer of fruit.

SMOKY DEVIL:

Substitute 2 ounces of a smoky mezcal like Creyente or Fidencio for the tequila.

BIG STAR

1531 N. DAMEN AVENUE
CHICAGO, IL 60622
773.235.4039
BIGSTARCHICAGO.COM

When this Alex Chilton fan heard about the delicious tacos coming from an always rocking taqueria and whiskey bar called Big Star in Chicago, I had to know if there was a connection to Chilton's band as much as I wanted to learn about the tacos and drinks served.

"We are big fans of the band and played their three LPs incessantly in the early days," explains Beverage Director Laurent Lebec. The nonstop spinning of vintage vinyl records from artists like Gram Parsons, Fleetwood Mac, and Alex Chilton is a big part of the restaurant's atmosphere and a definite draw for customers. The launch of the Big Star Recording Company in 2017 (a natural next step for any restaurant said no one ever) has shown that the owners' love of great music can morph into another worthy business.

When Chicago artist Tony Fitzpatrick created the restaurant's logo, he noted that a star is a symbol for unifying community. "That is a big part of the role we hope Big Star plays in Wicker Park and its second home in Wrigleyville," Lebec says. One look at the packed patio and lengthy line snaking from the Big Star TOGO Window makes it obvious that the restaurant's place in the community is firmly cemented.

Location had a lot to do with it. The former garage is near a busy intersection and train stop in a vibrant neighborhood. "The garage setting with working garage doors and an old sign pole to hang our logo was ideal for housing a honky-tonk, Mexican restaurant. Everything felt right when we were fortunate enough to be offered the lease in 2009," admits Lebec.

At Big Star, the tortillas are made fresh daily and the taco lineup changes every few months. Snag a Panza taco with crisp pork belly and chicharrón, or go vegetarian with a Yuba Guisado taco stuffed with guajillo-slathered tofu. "We do some seasonal changes, but also keep on staples like al pastor, pescado, and the walking taco," says Chef de Cuisine Chris Miller.

Whiskey is the highlighted spirit here, but Lebec says that in Big Star's early days, the tequila and mezcal list dialed in on a few distilleries. "We had Del Maguey from the jump in our margarita, along with tequila selections for El Tesoro, Lunazul, Herradura, Don Fulano, Arette, and a few others. We remained completely committed then as we do now to not carrying any mixtos. Our own tastes have changed; over the decade a lot has changed. We've got way more mezcals now, along with tequilas. We've done house barrels by the dozens, but we're still pretty focused, so as not to overwhelm." Lebec's Gold Dust Gimlet (page 123) is a Big Star tequila cocktail that certainly doesn't underwhelm.

BIG STAR GOLD DUST GIMLET SERVES 1

The folks at Big Star admit that they took "a very liberal approach" to this powerfully acidic cocktail classic with 1930s roots. They traded the usual gin for tequila and let the soothing '70s sounds of Fleetwood Mac inspire the cocktail's name. Beverage Director Laurent Lebec chimes in, "We added the complexity of grenadine to the usual formula to make this a totally different drink—rich with earthy sweetness, but a lot of floral notes as well."

1¾ ounces Herradura Blanco

¼ ounce St. George Raspberry Brandy

½ ounce Spiced Grenadine (*recipe follows*)

¼ ounce Marie Brizard CacaoBlanc

¾ ounce fresh lime juice

Grapefruit peel for garnish

WHAT'S IN A NAME?

Lauren Lebec explains, "I've named my cocktails all sorts of things! But because we play a lot of classic country, dusties, old rock, and lots of classic things, I've always felt a Fleetwood Mac–themed drink would be fitting. There's no gold in it, it's not particularly dusty, but Gold and Gimlet . . . well, it just rolls off the tongue! Visually the drink gets people to inquire as to what it is, and we find ourselves selling quite a few on color alone."

Combine everything in an ice-filled shaker tin. Pour into a rocks glass over fresh ice. Twist the grapefruit peel to express its aromatic oil and add to the glass as garnish.

SPICED GRENADINE:

Pour one 16-ounce bottle of pure pomegranate juice into a saucepan over low heat. Cook to reduce the liquid by ¼ to ⅓ of its original volume. Add 1 cup sugar. Stir to dissolve. Cook for a few minutes more, being careful not to let the liquid boil. Peel a whole orange into long strips using a wide peeler and avoiding the bitter white pith. Twist the peel strips over the saucepan to express their aromatic oils into the liquid and then drop the peels into the pan. Remove the pan from the heat and add a dash of orange flower water. Makes about 1¾ cups.

THE WALKING TACO SERVES 12

This is comfort food and convenience in one delicious package. Chef de Cuisine Chris Miller says that Big Star's "crazy good pinto bean dip made using three different types of chiles, onions, and garlic is spicy and super flavorful. Since we built The Walking Taco to cover all the culinary bases, we almost never have diners ask for add-ons or extras."

SPICY PINTO BEAN DIP

½ pound dry pinto beans

1 tablespoon vegetable oil

½ poblano chile pepper, roasted and peeled

¼ yellow onion, diced

5 garlic cloves, peeled and chopped

½ can Tecate beer

⅛ cup Cholula Hot Sauce

Salt to taste

12 (1-ounce) Frito bags

3 cups shredded Chihuahua cheese

¼ cup Mexican crema or sour cream

¼ cup Cholula Hot Sauce

¾ cup diced white onion

⅛ cup minced cilantro

1. Bring the beans to a boil with water to cover in a large pot over high heat. Reduce the heat to a simmer and cook until the beans are tender, about 1½ hours. Drain, reserving the cooking water.

2. Sauté the poblano, onion, and garlic in the vegetable oil in a large saucepan over medium heat for 5 minutes. Be careful not to burn the garlic.

3. Add the cooked beans, beer, and hot sauce to the pan. Pour in just enough of the reserved bean cooking water to cover the beans. Blend with a stick blender or mash with a potato masher. Season the beans with salt to taste.

4. Open each individual Frito bag and layer with the components, starting with ¼ cup of the bean dip, ¼ cup cheese, 1 teaspoon crema or sour cream, 1 teaspoon hot sauce, 1 tablespoon onion, and ½ teaspoon cilantro. Serve with a spoon for eating out of the bag.

EAST

THE RESTAURANTS

VIDA TACO BAR

200 MAIN STREET
ANNAPOLIS, MD 21401
443.837.6521
VIDATACOBAR.COM

It's perfectly fitting that the "flagship" of this farm-to-taco restaurant is in the Chesapeake Bay city that the U.S. Naval Academy calls home. And it's not surprising that two additional locations in Severna Park and Baltimore followed soon after. Fresh ingredients and a menu offering just drinks, appetizers, traditional and anything-but tacos entices in a fast-casual environment where service is a big part of the equation. But let's not forget the drinks. Happy hour is a big thing here and the offerings are from-scratch, juicy, and can be blended from an impressive assortment of tequila and mezcal. Live music is a part of the fabric of these communal gatherings, and a platform is given to both well-known local bands and up-and-coming high school bands to drive that community vibe home at every location.

Co-owner John Miller and Executive Chef Josh Brown pride themselves on keeping it local—a buzzword they back up by sourcing as many of the fresh, seasonal ingredients that they rely on from within a two-hundred-mile radius. Those fresh ingredients really stand out, especially in the toppings and garnishes—pickled purple cabbage, chipotle-tamari watermelon, house kimchi, and vinegary cherry bomb tomatoes—that embed Vida Taco Bar's offerings with uncommon flavor.

Though he has cooked a handful of times at the James Beard House in New York City and been recognized for his talents at the Charleston Food & Wine Festival, the self-taught Chef Brown admits he is in his element where something as basic as a tortilla or lettuce leaf can carry a world of flavor from plate to mouth for just a few bucks. Whether you like to keep it traditional with carne asada, house-made chorizo, and chicken tinga, or you like to live *la vida loca* and experience their Thai Basil Shrimp (page 132) or Vegan Bahn Mi taco, Vida Taco Bar's menu will meet you where you are and likely keep you coming back.

PURPLE DRANK SERVES 6

Forget wine and roses...wine and daisies seems to be a tipple trend. Vida Taco Bar's glowing cocktail is a customer favorite, but toss aside visions of those sad cough-syrup mixtures of the same name. This drink marries white and red wines with tequila and a splash of hibiscus liqueur for a flavorful, colorful ante up.

6 ounces fresh lime juice

6 ounces water

1½ ounce freshly squeezed orange juice

3 ounces organic agave nectar

3 ounces hibiscus liqueur

6 ounces red table wine

6 ounces Chablis

6 ounces blanco tequila

6 orange segments

6 orchid blossoms

1   Combine the lime juice, water, orange juice, agave nectar, hibiscus liqueur, red wine, Chablis, and tequila in a pitcher. Stir well. Refrigerate for 1 hour to chill thoroughly before serving.

2   Fill 6 highball glasses with crushed ice. Pour the chilled drink over the ice until the glasses are three-quarters full. Garnish with an orange segment and a flower blossom and serve with a straw.

THAI BASIL SHRIMP TACOS WITH GINGER PEANUT SAUCE MAKES 6

Don't be deterred by the lengthy ingredient list. This recipe comes together fast! I suggest wearing disposable gloves when handling the habanero, or you may learn that lesson the most memorable way. This peanut sauce makes a delicious cold noodle salad dressing—top with any leftover pickled vegetables and chopped cooked chicken.

SHRIMP

1 pound (21–25 count) shrimp, peeled and deveined

1 teaspoon smoked paprika

1 teaspoon kosher salt

½ teaspoon cayenne

2 teaspoons vegetable oil

PICKLED VEGETABLES

1 English cucumber, thinly sliced

1 carrot, peeled and thinly sliced

½ cup rice wine vinegar

2 tablespoons soy sauce

1½ tablespoons chopped fresh ginger

1 garlic clove, minced

2 tablespoons granulated sugar

1 tablespoon kosher salt

PICKLED RED ONIONS

1 red onion, thinly sliced

1 habanero pepper, minced

1 tablespoon kosher salt

½ tablespoon Mexican oregano

1½ cups lemon juice

6 warm corn or flour tortillas or Bibb lettuce leaves

Toppings: Thai basil leaves, Ginger-Peanut Sauce (*recipe follows*)

1   Toss the shrimp and all the seasonings in a bowl. Refrigerate until ready to cook.

2   Combine all the pickled vegetable ingredients in a bowl. Set aside to marinate at room temperature for at least 1 hour, and then refrigerate until ready to use.

3   Combine the pickled red onion ingredients in a bowl to marinate for at least 1 hour at room temperature and then refrigerate until ready to use.

4   Sear the shrimp in a large skillet in hot oil for 90 seconds on each side, or until cooked through. Remove from the heat.

5   Fill a warm tortilla with a spoonful each of the pickled vegetables and pickled red onions. Top with 3 shrimp per taco, and finish with a drizzle of the Ginger-Peanut Sauce and Thai basil leaves.

GINGER-PEANUT SAUCE MAKES 2½ CUPS

1 tablespoon sesame oil

¼ cup diced yellow onion

1 garlic clove, diced

1½ tablespoons chopped
  fresh ginger

1 teaspoon kosher salt

¼ cup Thai red curry paste

¼ cup lime juice

2 tablespoons soy sauce

1 tablespoon sugar

1 cup coconut milk

1 cup creamy peanut
  butter

1 Heat the sesame oil in a saucepan over medium heat. Add the onion, garlic, ginger and salt, and sweat the vegetables until the onions are translucent. Stir in the curry paste. Cook for 2 minutes. Deglaze the pan with lime juice.

2 Mix the soy sauce, sugar, and coconut milk into the curry mixture. Allow it to come to a boil over medium heat. Blend the mixture with a stick blender until smooth, or transfer to a regular blender and process until smooth. Blend the peanut butter into the curry mixture while it is still hot.

XACO TACO

370 RICHMOND STREET
PROVIDENCE, RI 02903
401.228.8286
XACOTACORI.COM

Xaco Taco is the brainchild of Rhode Island restaurateur John Elkhay and his restaurant group's executive chef Andy Pyle. Elkhay, culinary pro and mastermind behind successful restaurant concepts since the 1990s, had noticed during his travels around the world in recent years that Latin American food was ever-trending. He decided to harness the enthusiasm for it in a street taco concept back home in Rhode Island.

Xaco (pronounced *Zack-o*) is an original name Elkhay dreamed up to rhyme with "taco" and be catchy and fun. Fun is certainly the vibe you get inside the restaurant. "I wanted to re-create a street in Mexico, since we were going for a very authentically made taco, but using local inspiration," says Elkhay. He achieved it with street art, rusty signage, and, naturally, a taco truck. "We converted a 1977 Volkswagen Bus, trailered from Texas and made health department compliant. We use the bus for late-night tacos. It creates a lot of energy in the dining room," he explains. He didn't stop there. An eclectic mix of found objects has been enlisted into service: a recycled wagon serves as a table for twelve, a sauerkraut press was retooled to create an intimate table for four, and a four-man bobsled from the 1920s morphed into a stand-up cocktail area. Perhaps the best seats in the house—the 1950s foosball table that seats four and where you can actually play foosball while you eat.

In keeping with the farm-fresh philosophy the menu is a constant rotation of seasonal taco specials mixed in with the delicious taco standards. All are served on either house-made flour tortillas or traditional nixtamalized (page 15) corn tortillas made with white corn and lime, which sets Xaco Taco apart from many competitors. "Our greatest advantage is we make our taco shells to order from white corn. They're light and airy and the perfect foil to let the flavors inside the taco shine. Most places use premade commercial yellow corn that have too strong of a flavor and the wrong texture," explains Elkhay.

When the oyster harvest is in swing, the RI Oyster Tacos (page 137) are a menu mainstay. Around St. Paddy's Day, the Corned Beef Tacos are a hit. More traditional Mexican tacos also rotate in. Customers might stop in for the cheap tacos and funky atmosphere, but they come back again and again for the undeniable creativity and quality of the food that Chef Pyle serves . . . "Plus, we have the best cocktails in town!" says Elkhay.

DRUG MULE SERVES 1

This south-of-the-border spin on the Moscow Mule gets dosed with nutty-sweet amaretto and a few drops of CBD (cannabidiol) oil for relaxing measure or placebo effect. Owner John Elkhay admits he's a huge fan of the show *Breaking Bad*. "I saw an episode where the drug lords prayed to Jesús Malverde, and we have an idol inside the restaurant." Malverde, a mythical Robin Hood figure in Mexico, is often referred to as the Narco-Saint. Because both Moscow Mules and CBD oil are popular, Elkay suggested combining the two, and the Drug Mule was born. "Me being who I am, we tried five types of ginger beer and dozens of flavorings . . . and amaretto tasted best," explains Elkhay. Perhaps more than CBD, that unexpected ingredient elevates this mule to stud.

1½ ounce Mi Campo
   blanco tequila

½ ounce amaretto

5 milligrams CBD oil

3 ounces ginger beer

Juice of ½ lime

Lime wedge

Combine all the ingredients in a copper mule cup. Add ice and stir with a bar spoon. Garnish with a wedge of lime.

RI OYSTER TACOS SERVES 6 TO 8

Chef Pyle honors traditional techniques but innovates with local ingredients and regional flavors. This taco is rooted in tiny Rhode Island, which boasts two-dozen oyster farms, while its components all fit the formula for a great taco—protein, crunch, aromatics, something tart, something spicy, and something creamy. Speaking of Executive Chef Andy Pyle, owner John Elkhay says, "He has passion and understands the soul of Mexican food— a brilliant combination. He suggested the oyster, I'm like 'Really?' I didn't think it would work. To this day this is the best taco I've ever eaten."

1 quart vegetable oil

36 to 40 freshly shucked oysters or 2 (16 ounce) containers fresh oysters, drained

1 cup masa

1 cup all-purpose flour

5 tablespoons Xaco Spice (*recipe follows*)

24 fresh corn tortillas, warmed

Chipotle Crema (*recipe follows*)

1 cup salsa verde

¼ cup diced onions

Pickled Carrots (*recipe follows*)

Fresh cilantro sprigs

1. Heat about 1 inch of vegetable oil in a large Dutch oven until it reaches 350°F.

2. While the oil is heating, combine the masa, flour, and Xaco Spice in a bowl. Dredge the oysters in the mixture; shake off any excess.

3. Fry the oysters in batches for 3 to 4 minutes until golden on all sides. Drain on a layer of paper towels.

4. Place 3 fried oysters in a warm tortilla. Top with Chipotle Crema, salsa verde, diced onion, Pickled Carrots, and a sprinkle of fresh cilantro.

XACO SPICE

Combine 1 tablespoon each kosher salt, ground cumin, granulated garlic, paprika, and dried crushed chiles (Chef Pyle uses arbol and ancho chiles). Store in an airtight container and use within 6 weeks. Makes 5 tablespoons.

CHIPOTLE CREMA

Mince 1 to 2 canned chipotle chile peppers in adobo sauce and fold into 1 cup Mexican crema. Makes about 1 cup.

PICKLED CARROTS

Bring 1 cup white vinegar, 1 tablespoon kosher salt, 1 tablespoon granulated sugar, ½ bay leaf, and ¼ of a chopped habanero pepper to a boil in a small saucepan over medium-high heat. Remove the pan from the heat and pour the mixture over ½ pound julienned carrots.

THE BATANGA   SERVES 1

About an hour outside Guadalajara, in the town of Tequila, is a modest but glowing yellow cantina called La Capilla (The Chapel) on the corner of Juarez and Hidalgo streets. At this iconic bar, owner Don Javier Delgado Corona famously stirred his signature cocktail of tequila, lime, and Mexican Coca-Cola with his favorite salsa knife until he was well into his nineties. (His son does the stirring these days.) Don Javier created his Mexican-American mash-up in the 1960s and credits the slow stir with his well-used knife for the drink's magical qualities. It is sweet, tart, savory, and spirited—a fantastic formula for a great cocktail and also, it would appear, a very long life.

1 large lime

Rim salt

2 ounces blanco tequila

Mexican Coca-Cola
 (made with cane sugar)

Cut a wedge from the lime
and use it to dampen the rim
of a highball glass. Invert the
glass and twist it in rim salt to
coat. Squeeze the juice from
the rest of the lime into the
glass. Fill the glass with ice
and add the tequila. Top with
Mexican Coke, and then stir
with the knife you used to
slice the lime in Don Javier's
honor. Salud!

SWEET GRASS GRILL

24 MAIN STREET
TARRYTOWN, NY 10591
914.631.0000
SWEETGRASSGRILL.COM

David Starkey grew up on Manhattan's Upper East Side in a family that reveled in food and drink. His mother, a Nebraska native, loved to cook and entertain. "I have vivid memories of her standing at the dining room table cutting up a huge wheel of cheese for her food co-op." As an adult, David worked in television at CNN in New York, but he shared his mother's passion for hospitality and frequently hosted restaurant nights at home, replete with printed menus listing each course.

Fifteen years ago, he decided to trade the rat race of the city and his corporate job for a quieter life in the Hudson Valley. That first night in his new home he picked up takeout burritos to eat while unpacking boxes and found himself underwhelmed at first bite. He soon found out that there was a dearth of standout Mexican restaurants in town, so he went about creating one where he'd like to eat, and just like that his ERL (Eats Roots Leaves) Hospitality was born. The fast-casual Tomatillo in Dobbs Ferry was his first foray as restaurateur. He wanted a place that served artfully prepared Mexican dishes using ingredients sourced from Westchester County farmers who were raising responsibly and growing sustainably. This was back in 2004, when farm-to-table was barely a buzzword. David cheekily refers to the food served at Tomatillo as its own thing—authentic "Mexchester" cuisine.

Today, Executive Chef Juan Jimenez, a native of Puebla, Mexico, deftly designs the menus for ERL Hospitality, and runs the kitchen at their second venture, Sweet Grass Grill in Tarrytown. He weaves a bounty of imaginative vegetarian and vegan options in with the pasture-raised meats and sustainable seafood. The Jackfruit "Carnitas" Tacos (page 143) are spicy and sublime, with all the chile and spice you'd expect from classic pork carnitas but with none of the pig.

David explains that the focus on vegetarian food is less about personal health than the health of the planet. "I'm okay with eating meat when I know where my food is coming from, but over the years I've become more conscious about ingredients—I do not eat octopus or pork, but do fill up on bivalves like oysters because it is good for the environment. For me, it's about awareness, sustainability, and eating less for the environment's sake." Diners beware: It's hard to eat less here.

SWEET GRASS GRILL
MEZCAL MARGARITA   SERVES 1

This cocktail is the alchemy of the unexpected. Beverage Director Max Sears merges mezcal and cream sherry with beet, grapefruit, and orange juices that get sweetened with a spiced simple syrup. They call this a "margarita," but its complex earthiness and smoke puts it in its own category.

2 ounces Peloton de la Muerte mezcal

½ ounce Savory & James cream sherry

½ ounce beet juice

½ ounce grapefruit juice

¼ ounce fresh orange juice (or 1 orange slice, muddled)

½ ounce Brown Sugar–Cinnamon Simple Syrup (recipe follows)

1 dash El Guapo Polynesian Kiss Bitters

Thyme sprig (optional)

WHAT'S IN A NAME?

Owner David Sharkey was big on bison when he was brainstorming ideas for the restaurant. "Bison meat is sustainable and packs great protein and nutrients per pound," he says. Sweet Grass Grill is inspired by the sweet grasses that are the preferred forage for America's most iconic bovid.

Combine everything except the garnish in an ice-filled shaker tin. Shake vigorously. Strain into a rocks glass. Add ice. Garnish with a thyme sprig, if desired.

BROWN SUGAR–CINNAMON SIMPLE SYRUP:

Bring ¼ cup water to a simmer in a small saucepan. Add ¼ cup brown sugar, ¼ teaspoon ground cinnamon, ⅛ teaspoon cumin seeds, and ⅛ teaspoon whole allspice berries and whisk to dissolve the sugar. Remove from the heat and let steep for 4 to 5 minutes. Strain into a bottle and refrigerate up to 2 weeks. Makes about ⅓ cup.

JACKFRUIT "CARNITAS" TACOS SERVES 6

By looking at the photo on page 141, it's hard to tell that the pot of braised goodness is 100% vegan jackfruit, a fruit from a tree in the fig family. I've seen the ingredient on menus for years, but this gal was never enticed. My mind was blown when I tasted these tacos. The fruit simmers in a bath of flavorful aromatics and spices, and the end result is toothsome, tasty, and satisfies even a carnivore's craving for a meaty taco.

2 to 3 chipotles in adobo sauce

2 garlic cloves, chopped

1½ tablespoons smoked paprika

1¼ cups water

¼ cup tamari

1 tablespoon balsamic vinegar

1 tablespoon Frank's RedHot sauce

¼ cup olive oil

2 (10-ounce) cans jackfruit, drained and shredded

1 small white onion, sliced

2½ teaspoons whole cumin seeds

1 cinnamon stick

⅓ cup brown sugar

Corn tortillas

Chipotle Aioli (recipe follows)

Toppings: sliced avocado, shredded cabbage, chopped fresh cilantro, and sliced radishes

1 Preheat the oven to 400°F.

2 Combine the chipotles in adobo, garlic, and smoked paprika with a bit of the water. Add the tamari, balsamic, and hot sauce. Gently whisk in the oil, but do not emulsify.

3 Place the jackfruit, onions, cumin seeds, and cinnamon stick in a Dutch oven or lidded baking dish. Pour the liquid over the jackfruit, cover, and place in the middle of the oven. Cook for 90 minutes. Remove and let cool slightly before filling the tacos.

4 Spoon the jackfruit filling onto the bottom of a tortilla. Top with a drizzle of the Chipote Aioli. Layer with an avocado slice or two. Finish with some cabbage, chopped fresh cilantro, and a few radish slices.

CHIPOTLE AIOLI:

Combine 2 cups jarred Vegenaise, 1 garlic clove, 4 cilantro sprigs, 1 tablespoon fresh lemon juice, ½ chipotle chile in adobo sauce, 2 whole black peppercorns, and a generous pinch of salt in a mortar, and grind with a pestle until mashed and smooth. Makes about 2 cups.

LA ESQUINA—SOHO

114 KENMARE STREET
NEW YORK, NY 10012
646.613.7100
ESQUINANYC.COM

The hip and happening basement brasserie of the flagship La Esquina in SoHo is a loud, labyrinthine space that has amazed as much as its menu has enticed for over a dozen years. When it first opened, the owners were deliberate in the cultivation of an aura of mystery and exclusivity around what was happening downstairs. The phone number was unlisted and there was no clear signage, which left as many patrons confused as those in the know felt that they were in on the supersecret cues to get into the neighborhood's new cool club.

La Esquina means "the corner" and its neon sign glows the words "The Corner Deli." However, notices on the door that leads to the underground gathering place read "No Admittance" and "Employees Only." Those willing to buck rules and pass through the cautionary portal will find a vibrant place to perch with a top-shelf tequila or mezcal cocktail and watch the raucous, and quite often the recognizable, deliver air kisses to cheeks, snap selfies, and nosh on guac and chips while waiting for their plates to arrive.

If this thumping subterranean scene is not your thing, know that back outside on the corner you can order food to enjoy at sidewalk tables or take to-go from the brightly lit and clearly labeled taqueria window. Or, opt to dine in on larger plates at the sit-down, street-level café.

Classic tacos like bistec con queso—sliced ribeye served with salsa verde, cilantro, and Chihuahua cheese—carnitas, pollo, and pescado come wrapped in non-GMO corn tortillas or served atop a bevy of greens and veggies in a La Esquina Bowl. This is simple Mexican street food made from scratch with pristine ingredients. The meaty Hongos Tacos (page 146) marry earthy maitake mushrooms with a sweet corn puree, salsa roja, queso fresco, cilantro, and pumpkin seeds. It's a vegetarian taco full of in-your-face flavor that you'll want to order again and again. Wash your tacos down with a housemade margarita or Beverage Director, Inez Morcilio's complex Mucho Macho (page 145) with its smoke and spice.

MUCHO MACHO SERVES 1

Beverage Director Inez Morcilio created this bold mezcal cocktail that pairs beautifully with La Esquina's meaty mushroom taco.

2 ounces mezcal

½ ounce Cardamom Syrup (*recipe follows*)

1 dash orange bitters

2 dashes Angostura bitters

Orange zest curl

Combine the mezcal, Cardamom Syrup, and both bitters in a rocks glass. Add ice and stir. Garnish with an orange zest curl.

CARDAMOM SYRUP MAKES 1 QUART

4 tablespoons whole cardamom seeds

2 cups hot water

3 cups brown sugar

2 droppers of vanilla extract

1 Use a measuring cup to measure where 2 cups of water would fill a quart container. Mark with a piece of tape but do not fill with water.

2 Add the cardamom seeds into the quart container. Fill with hot water up to the tape line (2 cups) and immediately cover with a lid and let sit for 5 minutes.

3 Place the brown sugar into a large container. Use a strainer to pour the steeped hot water over the sugar and remove the cardamom seeds.

4 Stir. Stir. Stir. It may take a while for all the sugar to dissolve. Be patient.

5 Add 2 full droppers of vanilla into the mix and stir some more.

6 Pour the completely stirred mix back into the quart container.

LA ESQUINA HONGOS TACOS WITH CORN MOLE SERVES 2 TO 3

I can't get enough of these vegetarian tacos bursting with umami goodness. Like a steak, maitake mushrooms—also called Hen of the Woods—develop a flavorful crust when left undisturbed in a hot skillet for a few minutes to sear. Seasoned simply with salt and pepper, this taco filling is as easy as it gets. The corn *mole* (or sauce) is also a breeze to make. Just whirl the corn in a blender with a bit of its epazote-infused cooking water and ta-dah. It's a sauce that exemplifies how light of hand a cook can be when working with stellar ingredients.

4 ears of fresh corn, husks and silk removed

Leaves from 1 small epazote sprig

3 (3½-ounce each) maitake mushrooms

Olive oil

Kosher salt and freshly ground black pepper

6 (5-inch) corn tortillas, warmed

Toppings: salsa roja (optional), crumbled queso fresco, toasted pumpkin seeds, and chopped cilantro

1 Place the corn and epazote leaves in a large pot with water to cover and bring it to a boil over high heat. Reduce the heat to a simmer. Cook until the corn is tender, 5 to 8 minutes. Drain, reserving a bit of the cooking water.

2 Brush the mushrooms clean but do not rinse. Heat about 2 tablespoons olive oil in a large skillet over medium-high heat. Add the mushrooms and let sear, undisturbed, for 2 to 3 minutes to develop a nice brown crust on one side. Begin to sauté, adjusting the heat so as not to burn, until golden brown and just tender, 3 to 5 minutes more. Season with salt and freshly ground black pepper.

3 Slice the kernels off the cooked corn cobs. Add the kernels to a high-speed blender and blend to a sauce-like consistency, adding a bit of the reserved cooking water as needed to create a corn mole.

4 Divide the sautéed mushrooms among the tortillas. Spoon a bit of the corn mole over the mushrooms. Top with a bit of salsa roja, if desired, queso fresco crumbles, pumpkin seeds, and chopped cilantro.

TRAIL BREAK TAPS & TACOS

129 S MAIN STREET
WHITE RIVER JUNCTION, VT 05001
802.281.3208
TRAILBREAKWRJ.COM

If the taco-munching surfers of Southern California were teleported to Trail Break Taps & Tacos at the base of a snowy mountain ski resort in Vermont, they'd be stoked. Guaranteed, the laid-back vibe, nods to outdoor sporting life, and uncommonly delicious tacos would have them swapping surfboards for snowboards and making plans to stick around for a while. Owner and California native Topher Lyons and Chef Dennis Marcoux have created an atmosphere and menu that draws crowds. It's a place outdoor adventurers, retirees, families, and hipsters come to congregate at the end of the day to enjoy great grub served in a welcoming atmosphere.

At Trail Break you can enjoy an array of epic dishes on the patio while seated inside an old four-seater gondola that used to hang from the ski lift above the slopes at Killington Resort. Inside, a bright kaleidoscope of sky blue, mountain green, and sunset orange accent walls, and furnishings match the space with the warmth of place. The menu is divided by "verticals" (the burritos) and "horizontals" (the tacos), including a handful of what they categorize as "tacky tortillas" (the quesadillas). Inventive taco offerings like pork belly, Brussels sprouts, and papaya salsa or fried ocean perch served with cilantro slaw and sour mango chow chow make diners salivate. Their Chorizo-Spiced Tuna and Avocado Taco (page 150) deserves a permanent place in your recipe box. Make them in miniature to serve as your next two-bite cocktail party appetizer and you'll be destined for host stardom.

While beer on tap is a big part of what Trail Break delivers to thirsty guests, the cocktails aren't an afterthought. From garnish to glass and every gulp of liquid inside, the drinks entice. House-made agua frescas, on-tap kombucha, and Mexican and artisan sodas slake teetotaler thirsts, but also weave their way into some pretty impressive cocktails like a flavorful rotation of Gnargaritas or the flaming Hot Box Time Machine, a New England-meets-the tropics bowl for two made with Vermont-distilled maple whiskey, local ginger-beer shandy, exotic juices from distant lands, spices and bitters. Their Prickly Pear Paloma (page 149) keeps things simple with just four ingredients, but it tastes anything but.

PRICKLY PEAR PALOMA SERVES 1

I drink my weight in seltzer most days and rarely sip sodas anymore, but I'd give you a case of Fresca for one Jarritos grapefruit soda any day. Like Mexican Coca-Cola, Jarritos grapefruit soda is made with pure cane sugar. It has a pleasing yin and yang of sweetness and citrus. Now to the cocktail . . . when Topher and Dennis sent this recipe, it seemed like it would be cloyingly sweet, but it's a balanced, blushing paloma with hints of smokiness in every sip. Find the prickly pear syrup on Amazon and use whatever gummy grapefruit candy makes you salivate.

1¾ ounce Vida Mezcal

¼ ounce Cheri's Desert Harvest Prickly Pear Cactus Syrup

Jarritos grapefruit soda

Sour gummy grapefruit candy

Pour the mezcal and prickly pear syrup in an ice-filled pint glass. Top with the grapefruit soda and stir gently with a bar spoon. Garnish with sour gummy grapefruit candy.

CHORIZO-SPICED TUNA AND AVOCADO TACO

MAKES ABOUT 4 TACOS

Follow the dogma of taco authenticity and you'll miss out on this divine Trail Break taco that combines a nest of fried potato shreds, nuggets of tender sushi-grade tuna and buttery avocado, and a duo of sauces with creative aplomb. This is one taco I will make again and again. This filling is also terrific tucked into a Nori Taco Shell (page 42).

Canola oil

1 russet potato, peeled, shredded

Kosher salt and freshly ground black pepper

1 pound raw sushi-grade tuna

1 ripe avocado

¼ cup Red Adobo Sauce (*recipe follows*)

4 warm flour or corn tortillas

Spicy Crema (*recipe follows*)

Micro cilantro or chopped cilantro

1 Bring 1 inch of canola oil to 350°F in a cast-iron skillet. Squeeze excess moisture from the shredded potatoes by wringing in a clean kitchen towel. Fry the potatoes in the hot oil for about 2 minutes or until golden brown. Remove with a slotted spoon to drain on a plate lined with paper towels. Season lightly with salt and pepper.

2 Finely dice the tuna and avocado into ⅛-inch pieces. Toss with the Red Adobo Sauce. Set aside.

3 Arrange a bit of the fried potato in the center of a warm tortilla. Top with the tuna-avocado mixture. Top with a drizzle of the Spicy Crema and cilantro leaves.

RED ADOBO SAUCE MAKES ABOUT 6½ CUPS

1 cup ancho chile powder

16 garlic cloves, peeled

2 teaspoons ground cinnamon

1 teaspoon ground black pepper

½ teaspoon ground cumin

2 teaspoons Mexican oregano

¾ cup apple cider vinegar

½ cup salt

4¼ cups water

Bring all ingredients to a boil in a saucepan. Once boiling, turn off the heat. Remove the saucepan from the heat and let cool to room temperature. Puree ingredients in a blender. Cool completely.

SPICY CREMA
MAKES ABOUT 4½ CUPS

- 5 dried New Mexico chile peppers
- 2 cups boiling water
- 1 tablespoon rice wine vinegar
- 4 cups mayo
- 2 tablespoons salt
- 1 tablespoon freshly ground black pepper
- Juice of 4 oranges
- ¼ teaspoon xantham gum (optional)

Place the chiles in the boiling water. Turn off the heat and let the chiles soak for at least 1 hour. Drain, reserving the soaking liquid. Remove the stems from the peppers and place the peppers in a blender with the remaining ingredients (note: xanthan gum acts as an all-natural thickener that stabilizes the sauce). Begin blending on low speed, gradually increasing to high speed to puree. Add the reserved soaking liquid as needed to reach desired consistency. Taste and adjust the seasoning as needed.

THE AMERICAN DESSERT TACO

The tinny, melodic minstrel music that has served as the harbinger of frosty treats rolling down the street has changed little over the half century that ice cream trucks have been on the road. Surprisingly, ice cream truck menus haven't changed all that much either. You still can get a chewy fudge pop, syrupy snow cone, or rock-hard Drumstick—what the Trail Break (page 148) guys would label the "vertical" to the horizontal dessert taco. The Choco Taco was the brainchild of Alan Drazen, a former Good Humor ice cream man and a newly minted manager at rival Jack & Jill in the early '80s. Mexican food was trending big-time then, and Drazen had noticed that Jack & Jill didn't have any special novelty products of their own. He dreamed up an ice cream take on the taco and, as they say, "The rest is history!" The Choco Taco became an ice cream truck hit long before it became a mainstream drive-thru window delight at Taco Bell. It remains a nostalgic summertime, or anytime, treat that restaurants and pastry chefs have riffed on, retooled, and embellished ever since. The dessert taco here gets amped up a bit with Mexican flavors—cinnamon in a tuile cookie shell, a dulce de leche drizzle, and a sprinkle of toasted almonds for crunch. You might also call it the Dreamboat.

HONEY-CINNAMON DESSERT TACOS MAKES 12 TACOS

The batter for the shells thickens as it cools, so the bake time increases for later batches, thus the range.

HONEY-CINNAMON TACO SHELLS

¼ cup butter

⅓ cup granulated sugar

⅓ cup honey

¼ teaspoon salt

½ cup all-purpose flour

½ teaspoon cinnamon

2 cups chocolate ice cream

½ cup dulce de leche

½ cup chopped salt-roasted almonds

1 Preheat the oven to 350°F.

2 Combine the butter, sugar, and honey in a medium saucepan and stir over medium heat until there are no sugar granules left, about 3 minutes. Remove from the heat and whisk in the salt, flour, and cinnamon.

3 Spoon 1 tablespoon of the batter onto a parchment-lined baking sheet (spoon batter for no more than 2 cookies per baking sheet as they will spread!). Bake for 3 to 6 minutes, or until the cookies have spread and are a light golden brown.

4 Let cool for 1 minute and then use a spatula to drape the cookies over a rolling pin set over a sheet tray to create a taco-shell shape. Let cookies cool completely.

5 Freeze cookies for 30 minutes before filling.

6 Scoop ¼ cup ice cream in each taco shell. Drizzle each with 1 tablespoon dulce de leche and a sprinkle of 1 tablespoon chopped almonds. Serve immediately.

RESOURCES

BOOKS

- Arellano, Gustavo. *Taco USA: How Mexican Food Conquered America.* New York: Scribner, 2012.

- Bullock, Tom. *The Mezcal Experience: A Field Guide to the World's Best Mezcals and Agave Spirits.* London: Jacqui Small, 2017.

- Deseran, Sara. *Tacolicious: Festive Recipes for Tacos, Snacks, Cocktails, and More.* Berkeley, CA: Ten Speed Press, 2014.

- Janzen, Emma. *Mezcal: The History, Craft & Cocktails of the World's Ultimate Artisanal Spirit.* Minneapolis, MN: Voyageur Press, 2017.

- Moore, Lindsey, and Jennifer Boudinot. *Viva Mezcal: Mixing, Sipping & Other Adventures with Mexico's Original Handcrafted Spirit.* Sydney, Australia: Weldon Owen, 2018.

- Schroeder, James. *Understanding Mezcal.* Chicago: Prensa Press, 2019.

- Schumann, Charles. *The American Bar: The Artistry of Mixing Drinks.* New York: Abbeville Press, 1995.

- Stupak, Alex, and Jordana Rothman. *Tacos: Recipes and Provocations.* New York: Clarkson Potter, 2015.

FILM

- *Taco Chronicles*, Netflix (2019)

- *Agave is Life*, ArcheoProductions Inc. (2014)

WEBSITES

- www.tequilainterchangeproject.org
- www.tequila.net
- www.liquor.com
- www.theculturetrip.com
- www.diffordsguide.com
- www.thrillist.com
- www.foodandwine.com
- www.drinks.seriouseats.com
- www.mezcalphd.com
- www.smithsonianmag.com

ACKNOWLEDGMENTS

I am indebted to the many talented people at Tiller Press and Simon & Schuster for taking on this Spirited Pairings series at a time when hearing the word "yes" meant everything. To publisher Theresa DiMasi and executive editor Anja Schmidt, thank you for sticking your necks out and, volume by volume, giving singular focus to my all-over-the-place ideas. A shout-out to Ian King and Matthew Michelman for dotting *I*s, crossing *T*s, and tallying the important numbers. My glass is raised to creative director Patrick Sullivan for his beautiful cover art, and Matt Ryan—your never-ending design creativity and on-set direction is priceless and your trajectory has been fun to watch, and to Kayley Hoffman and Stacey Sakal for giving clarity to my copy. Clink-clink to PR and marketing powerhouses Marlena Brown, Scottie Ellis, Erica Magrin, Sam Ford, and Jay Strell for making this book stand out in a sea of others. To my point person Samantha Lubash—know that I understand the hard work you do and am thankful you make sure all the fillings stay in the taco.

Gratitude goes to the numerous restaurant managers and PR folks who helped line up interviews and secured recipes to test—Andrea Moreno, Annie Goldenberg, Casey Moore, David Starkey, David Yusen, Eliza Harlan, Eric Vasquez, Jenna Lorenz, Lindsey Brown, Lizzie Williams, Lydia Russo, Marel Holler Hanners, Melissa Michel, Quinn Collins, Thien-Y Hoang, and Vincent Ventura.

To my husband, John, and our daughters, Parker, Ella, and Adeline, and so many friends who never tired of my tacos-in-testing or "try this . . ." tequila tipples: I am forever grateful for your gluttony in the name of my deadlines. To my idol and big sister, Rebecca, and Venezuelan brother Carlos Briceño: thanks for turning my summer of work in New Mexico into the best kind of party. Laura Ruiz, thank you for being a part of our lives, being my sounding board, and a dear friend. To culinary pro Antonia Allegra, Rancho La Puerta matriarch Deborah Szekely, and my San Francisco sister and mentor Tori Ritchie, thank you for sharing that epiphanic night at Asao in Tecate, Mexico, and for the many delicious days on the ranch. Lyda Jones Burnette, you are a godsend and the recipe tester of testers. I could not have produced book one or two in less than twelve weeks without you. Ferrell Carter, it is so fun to see your passion for food and publishing. Your contributions to this book are immense and delicious. Lastly, to my Blueline Creative Group collaborators—Becky Luigart-Stayner, Mindi Shapiro, Torie Cox, Ellie Stayner, Gordon Sawyer, and Jestina Howard—your hard work and insane talents make the process fun and everything you touch beautiful. Though it may sound like I emptied it, I can assure all listed here that my margarita glass overflows!

METRIC CHART

The recipes that appear in this cookbook use the standard United States method for measuring liquid and dry or solid ingredients (teaspoons, tablespoons, and cups). The information on this page is provided to help cooks outside the U.S. successfully use these recipes. All equivalents are approximate.

METRIC EQUIVALENTS FOR DIFFERENT TYPES OF INGREDIENTS

A standard cup measure of a dry or solid ingredient will vary in weight depending on the type of ingredient. A standard cup of liquid is the same volume for any type of liquid. Use the following chart when converting standard cup measures to grams (weight) or milliliters (volume).

STANDARD CUP	FINE POWDER (ex. flour)	GRAIN (ex. rice)	GRANULAR (ex. sugar)	LIQUID SOLIDS (ex. butter)	LIQUID (ex. milk)
1	140 g	150 g	190 g	200 g	240 ml
¾	105 g	113 g	143 g	150 g	180 ml
⅔	93 g	100 g	125 g	133 g	160 ml
½	70 g	75 g	95 g	100 g	120 ml
⅓	47 g	50 g	63 g	67 g	80 ml
¼	35 g	38 g	48 g	50 g	60 ml
⅛	18 g	19 g	24 g	25g	30 ml

USEFUL EQUIVALENTS FOR DRY INGREDIENTS BY WEIGHT

(To convert ounces to grams, multiply the number of ounces by 30.)

OZ	LB	G
1 oz	¹⁄₁₆ lb	30 g
4 oz	¼ lb	120 g
8 oz	½ lb	240 g
12 oz	¾ lb	360 g
16 oz	1 lb	480 g

USEFUL EQUIVALENTS FOR LENGTH

(To convert inches to centimeters, multiply the number of inches by 2.5.)

IN	FT	YD	CM	M
1 in			2.5 cm	
6 in	½ ft		15 cm	
12 in	1 ft		30 cm	
36 in	3 ft	1 yd	90 cm	
40 in			100 cm	1 m

USEFUL EQUIVALENTS FOR LIQUID INGREDIENTS BY VOLUME

TSP	TBSP/PT/QT	CUPS	FL OZ	ML	L
¼ tsp				1 ml	
½ tsp				2 ml	
1 tsp				5 ml	
3 tsp	1 Tbsp		½ fl oz	15 ml	
	2 Tbsp	⅛ cup	1 fl oz	30 ml	
	4 Tbsp	¼ cup	2 fl oz	60 ml	
	5⅓ Tbsp	⅓ cup	3 fl oz	80 ml	
	8 Tbsp	½ cup	4 fl oz	120 ml	
	10⅔ Tbsp	⅔ cup	5 fl oz	160 ml	
	12 Tbsp	¾ cup	6 fl oz	180 ml	
	16 Tbsp	1 cup	8 fl oz	240 ml	
	1 pt	2 cups	16 fl oz	480 ml	
	1 qt	4 cups	32 fl oz	960 ml	
			33 fl oz	1000 ml	1 l

USEFUL EQUIVALENTS FOR COOKING/OVEN TEMPERATURES

	FAHRENHEIT	CELSIUS	GAS MARK
Freeze Water	32° F	0° C	
Room Temperature	68° F	20° C	
Boil water	212° F	100° C	
	325° F	160° C	3
	350° F	180° C	4
	375° F	190° C	5
	400° F	200° C	6
	425° F	220° C	7
	450° F	230° C	8
Broil		Grill	

INDEX

Art: Paul Ware

ABOUT THE AUTHOR

KATHERINE COBBS is a writer, editor, and culinary professional with twenty-five years of experience. She is also the author of *Cookies & Cocktails,* the first book in this Guide to Spirited Pairings series. She has collaborated with country music star Martina McBride on two cookbooks—*Around the Table* and *Martina's Kitchen Mix,* produced books for multiple James Beard Award—winning chefs, and most recently worked with Pulitzer Prize—winner and *New York Times* bestselling author Rick Bragg on *My Southern Journey,* *TODAY* show contributor Elizabeth Heiskell on the bestselling *What Can I Bring?* cookbook and *The Southern Living Party Cookbook,* Southern gentleman Matt Moore on *The South's Best Butts,* Texas author and sommelier Jessica Dupuy on *United Tastes of Texas* and *United Tastes of the South,* and soulful Atlanta chef Todd Richards on his critically acclaimed *SOUL* cookbook.